THECAGED**RHYTHM**
GUITARMETHOD

Learn to Play Any Chord Anywhere on the Neck Using The CAGED System

ROB**GARLAND**

FUNDAMENTAL**CHANGES**

The CAGED Rhythm Guitar Method

Learn to Play Any Chord Anywhere on the Neck Using The CAGED System

ISBN: 978-1-78933-416-6

Published by www.fundamental-changes.com

www.fundamental-changes.com

For over 350 free guitar lessons with videos check out:

www.fundamental-changes.com

Join our free Facebook Community of Cool Musicians

www.facebook.com/groups/fundamentalguitar

Tag us for a share on Instagram: **FundamentalChanges**

Cover Image Copyright: Shutterstock, Robert Kirby

Contents

About the Author

Rob Garland grew up in Kent, England. He worked in a diverse array of bands and played on the London college circuit. He later performed hundreds of gigs at festivals and clubs throughout the U.S. with his band The Blue Monks, opening for artists such as B.B. King, Booker T. and Chuck Berry.

He now lives in Los Angeles, where he continues to write and record his original music, ranging from jazz-fusion instrumentals to acoustic vocal songs, which are available to stream/download. He regularly performs at clubs such as The Baked Potato, Alva's Showroom and The Mint. He has recorded sessions at studios such as The Village Recorder, Revolver and J.J. Abrams' Bad Robot.

Rob has been teaching guitar for over 25 years. He has taught hundreds of private students, created best-selling instructional courses for TrueFire and JamPlay, written books for Cherry Lane, and has served on the guitar faculty at Musicians Institute in Hollywood. Currently he is a guitar mentor for Sonora Guitar Intensive and his most recent eBook is entitled *Guitar Play! Motivation & Practice*.

Rob has performed with musicians including Steve Vai, Jimmy Haslip (The Yellowjackets), Marco Minnemann (Joe Satriani), Gus Thornton (Albert King), Joel Taylor (Allan Holdsworth) and Tony Newton (Gary Moore).

He is endorsed by Bogner amplifiers, Xotic guitars, James Tyler guitars, Curt Mangan strings, Moody Straps and ChickenPicks. He is also a consultant for Blink, a music education platform.

Rob loves music and the guitar as much as he did when he was 14 – possibly even more now. He says, "I'm fascinated by the harmony of jazz combined with the energy and tone of rock!"

Visit him at **https://www.robgarland.net** and on social media.

Introduction

Having taught hundreds of guitarists over the years, I've noticed that many players focus on their lead playing but don't spend nearly as much time developing their rhythm guitar chops. This is unfortunate, because when we guitarists venture out into the real world, the majority of our time is spent playing rhythm guitar! However, fret not (pun intended), for the solution to this problem is in your hands.

In this book, we're going to use the CAGED system to improve and expand your rhythm playing into new areas. By applying the ideas here, you'll first gain a confident, practical understanding of the tools you need for expressive rhythm playing. You'll also learn how to play chords (and therefore songs) all over the fretboard using triads, just like the pros.

Second, as well as increasing your fretboard knowledge, this rhythmic journey will blur the lines between rhythm and lead playing (in a good way), as you learn how to combine major, minor and dominant 7th chords and play common chord sequences, adding embellishments such as double-stops and single note fills.

If you're new to the CAGED system, what is it and how do we use it?

In simple terms, CAGED is a way of taking the open chord shapes we learned when we first picked up the guitar, and moving them up/down the neck, enabling us to play the same chord in several different places on the fretboard. But this definition doesn't do justice to the way in which experienced guitar players can fully utilize CAGED.

If you learn to play chords on different string sets, and use inversions to make your chord voicings sound more connected, you will be able to freely express yourself when playing a wide range of popular song forms – just like an improvising soloist.

So, whether you're playing in a band or jamming at home, this essential guide will help take your rhythm playing to the next level. In time, it will also eliminate the need for you to carry around a chord dictionary in your gig bag. I hope it will inspire you with a fresh respect and love for all things rhythm guitar!

Let's dig in!

Rob

Get the Audio

The audio files for this book are available to download for free from **www.fundamental-changes.com.** The link is in the top right-hand corner. Simply select this book title from the drop-down menu and follow the instructions to get the audio.

We recommend that you download the files directly to your computer, not to your tablet, and extract them there before adding them to your media library. You can then put them on your tablet or smart phone. On the download page, there is a help PDF, and we also provide technical support via the contact form.

For over 350 free guitar lessons with videos check out:

www.fundamental-changes.com

Join our free Facebook Community of Motivated Musicians

www.facebook.com/groups/fundamentalguitar

Tag us for a share on Instagram: **FundamentalChanges**

Chapter One: Identifying CAGED Major Chords

Let's begin by taking a look at some familiar major chords and learn how to play them using the CAGED system.

The word CAGED describes the five chord shapes used in this system. Think back to when you first picked up the guitar and played open C, A, G, E and D chords. Those are the shapes that make up CAGED. Let's start with a simple D major chord and work it through the system, playing the shapes in order.

CAGED C Shape

The first chord shape in the CAGED system is the C shape. Let's look at how we can play a D major chord using this shape.

When we play a C chord in the open position, the first and third strings are played open. To create a moveable version of this shape, we need to use our first finger as a "poor man's capo" to barre those strings.

To play a "C shape" D major, we move the shape up to where the root note (D) is located on the fifth string, 5th fret (indicated by a square note on the diagram below), with the first finger barring at the 2nd fret.

Being able to visualize the CAGED shapes is important, so take a moment and look at how the C shape has been transformed into a D chord.

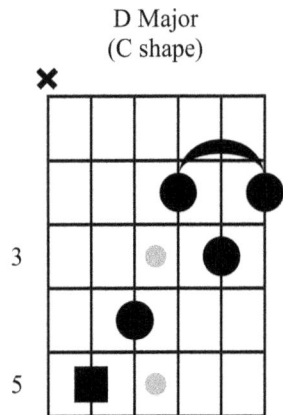

D Major
(C shape)

Example 1a:

Don't worry if this chord voicing initially feels a little awkward to play. It's important to understand how the chords are formed, but you'll soon see that the real magic of CAGED lies in the smaller chord voicings that exist *inside* these bigger shapes.

CAGED A Shape

The second chord shape in the CAGED system is the A shape. Let's apply it to the D major chord.

When we play an A chord in the open position, the first and fifth strings are played open. We normally play an open A chord with our first, second and third fingers, but to make the shape moveable, our first finger becomes a barre, and the rest of the notes are played with the second, third and fourth fingers.

To play D major using the A shape, the first finger barres the 5th fret, beginning from the root note (D) on the fifth string.

You're probably familiar with this shape as a standard major barre chord with its root on the fifth string. In the past, you may have used just your third or fourth finger to barre the notes on the middle strings. Visualize how the open A chord shape has been moved up the neck to play this D chord.

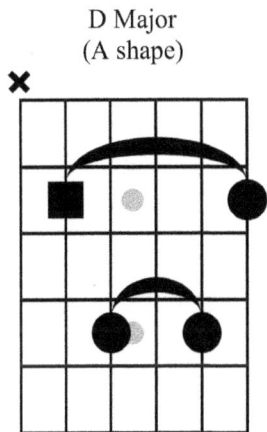

D Major
(A shape)

Example 1b:

CAGED G Shape

The third chord shape is the G shape.

This one can appear a little intimidating to play at first glance, because it looks like an awkward stretch, but don't worry – the most important thing at this stage is to be able to visualize the shape, so that when we begin to extract smaller shapes from it, you'll understand where they come from.

When you play an open G chord, you may use your first and fourth fingers on the fifth/first strings respectively, then stretch your second finger over to play the sixth string bass note.

Alternatively, like me, you can fret the sixth string root with the third finger and play the note on the fifth with the second finger. Doing it this way makes it easier to then move the G shape around the fretboard, as your first finger is freed up to make a barre.

In the open position the first finger isn't needed, but to play a D major chord with the G shape we use it to barre the second, third and fourth strings at the 7th fret.

Don't stress if you can't get this chord to sound completely clean to begin with, just look at the way the G shape from the open position is now used to play a D chord.

D Major
(G shape)

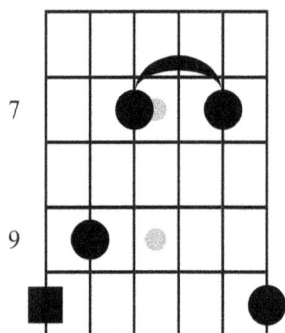

Example 1c:

CAGED E Shape

The fourth CAGED shape is one I'm sure you've played before – the E shape. You may not have thought of this shape as being related to the open E chord, but you will from now on!

To make the E shape moveable, the first finger is used to barre all the strings. The D root note is located at the 10th fret on the sixth string, so we barre across all the strings at the 10th. Take a moment to see that you're playing an open E chord shape in your familiar barre chord.

D Major
(E shape)

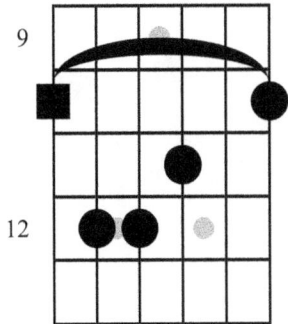

Example 1d:

CAGED D Shape

The fifth and final CAGED shape is the D shape.

Since we're demonstrating the CAGED shapes with a D major chord, we'll play it at the 12th fret, so you can better visualize the moveable version.

To fret the part of the shape that looks like an open D chord, use your second, fourth and third fingers on the third, second and first strings respectively. When we play an open D chord, the fourth string is played open, but in the moveable shape your first finger plays the root note on the fourth string.

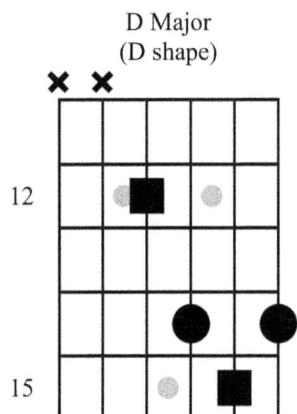

D Major
(D shape)

Example 1e:

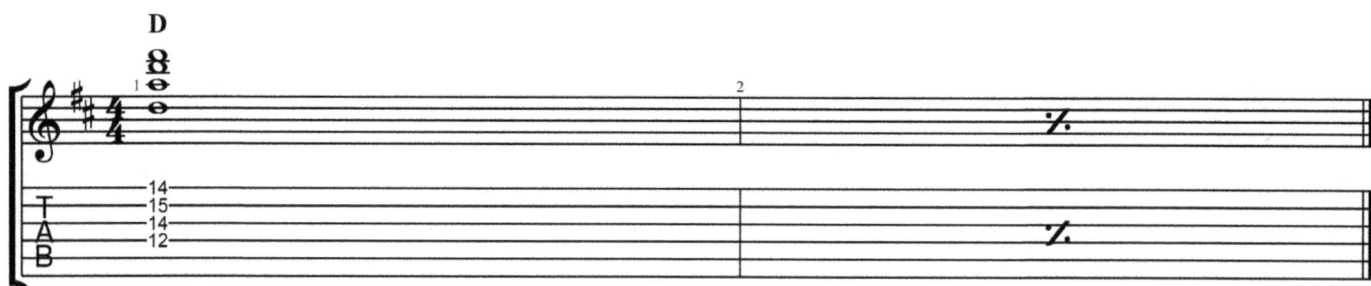

Finding Inversions Within the Shapes

So far, we've played a D major chord in five positions on the fretboard and covered a wide range of the neck using the CAGED shapes. Next, we're going to investigate the musical gems hiding in plain sight within these CAGED shapes.

CAGED C Shape: root triad and inversions

Let's return to the CAGED "C shape" for D major, but this time break it down into smaller shapes across groups of three strings. All of these smaller shapes exist *inside* the larger shape – we're just separating them into smaller units.

D major is constructed using the notes D, F# and A (in order, the root, 3rd and 5th intervals of the chord).

If we play just three notes from the CAGED shape beginning on the fifth string root note, we form a D triad (D, F#, A).

Now, if we move across a string and play the next three notes beginning from the fourth string, we form an *inversion* of D major (a D major chord where the D is not the lowest note played). Here, the note order is F#, A, D.

On the sheet music for a song, this chord is often written as D/F#. In other words, a D major chord with an F# in the bass. This shape crops up in some rock-tastic songs by bands like Queen, Free and The Rolling Stones. A D major chord with the 3rd as the lowest note is known as a *first inversion*.

If we move over another string to play the next group of three notes, we get a *second inversion* (a chord in which the 5th is the lowest note). Here, the note order is A, D, F#. This handy movable D triad on the top three strings is ideal for intros and second guitar parts.

Play through these shapes in Example 1f. Play only the three notes that make up the chord and mute the other strings when strumming/picking.

Note that you'll now need to use different fingers to play these shapes, compared to the larger version. Practice jumping between the smaller shapes and mix up the order. The skill you're developing here is to become fluent in switching between small voicings, all the while visualizing the larger shape they came from.

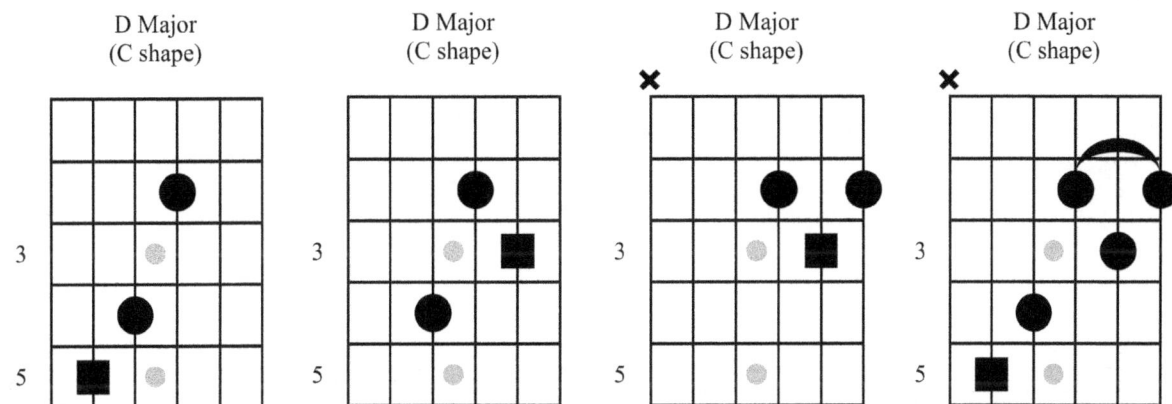

Example 1f:

CAGED A Shape: power chord, root triad and inversions

Let's apply the same idea to the CAGED A shape and play smaller D chord voicings on groups of three strings.

If we play the chord from its root note on the fifth string and add the fourth and third strings we get a D5 chord, also known as a "power chord" (a common rock voicing that contains no 3rd). I'm sure the 15-year-old kid in you already knows this chord voicing!

Barring the second, third and fourth strings at the 7th fret gives us a second inversion, with the 5th (A) as the lowest note. This voicing is useful for faux slide parts and Richie Blackmore style rock rhythm.

The root triad begins on the third string. This is a perfect voicing for shimmering pop-rock. You'll find examples utilized by bands such as U2 and The Police. Plug in your chorus and delay pedals!

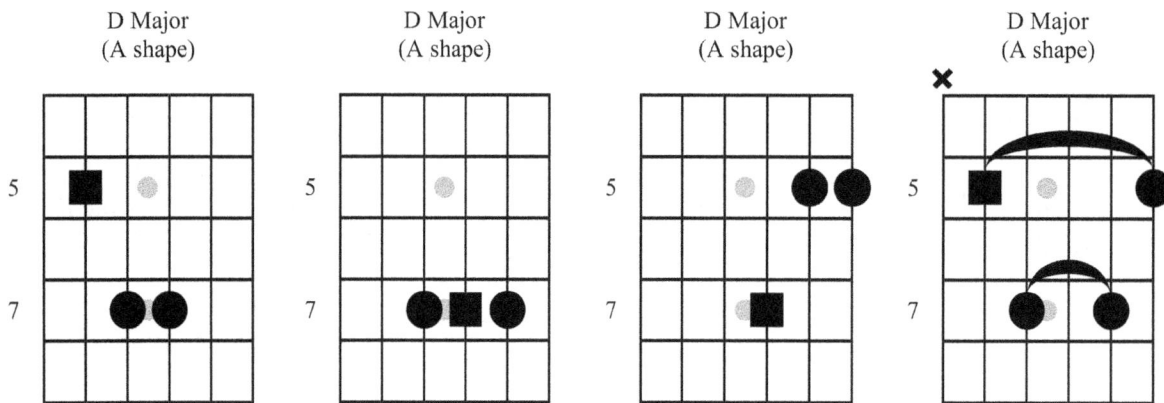

D Major (A shape)   D Major (A shape)   D Major (A shape)   D Major (A shape)

Example 1g:

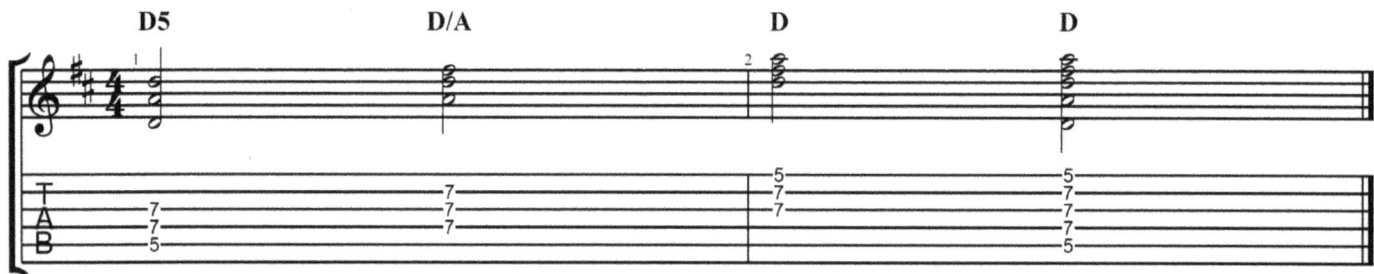

Combining CAGED C and A shapes

The magic of CAGED starts to happen when we begin to combine shapes. Let's take the C and A shapes for D major, combine them, and add some simple embellishments. In the next chapter, we'll look at where such embellishments come from, but for now, just think about how the C and A shapes are located next to each other on the fretboard. Practice moving between these two shapes, using the small fragments we've practiced. Here are two examples to get you started.

D Major
(C shape)

D Major
(A shape)

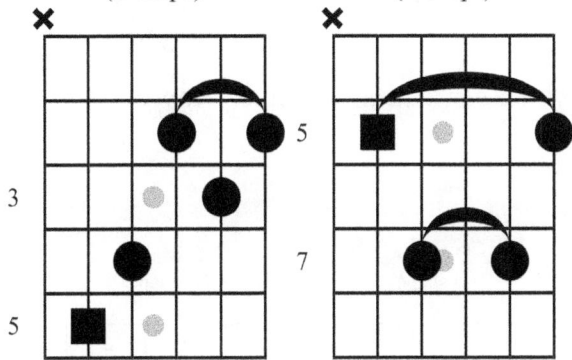

Example 1h:

Example 1i:

let ring - - - - - - -

CAGED G Shape: root triad and inversions

Next, let's examine the CAGED G shape.

If we begin by playing a D chord from its root note on the sixth string and add the fifth and fourth string notes we form a D triad from the lower part of the G shape.

When we play the next three-string group, starting from the fifth string, we form a first inversion with the 3rd (F#) in the bass. This is a popular voicing as it allows you to slide between the CAGED A and G shapes, connecting them. Think Jimi Hendrix, John Frusciante or John Mayer, depending on when you were born.

Barring the second, third and fourth strings at the 7th fret gives us a second inversion (the same one we just played in the CAGED A shape, with the 5th (A) as the lowest note). This voicing is the go-between for CAGED A and G shapes and marks the place where they intersect.

Finally, the top three strings contain a root-3rd-root voicing, which can add a nice funky top end to your rhythm parts. Just ask The Jackson 5.

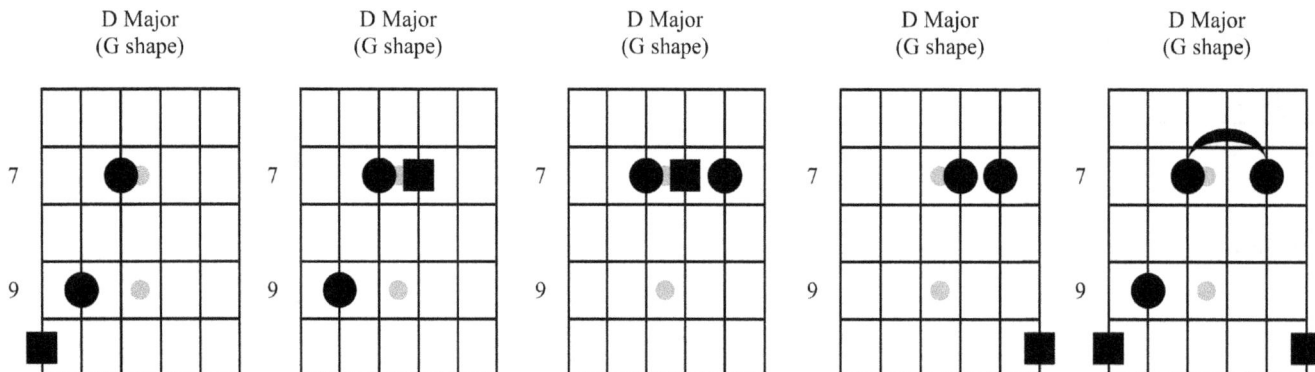

D Major (G shape)   D Major (G shape)   D Major (G shape)   D Major (G shape)   D Major (G shape)

Example 1j:

CAGED E Shape: power chord, root triad and inversions

Although the CAGED E shape may be familiar to you, there are some useful three string voicings lurking within it that you may not have experimented with.

If we begin by playing the chord from its root note on the sixth string, we get a D5 power chord. Voiced here, this is ideal for Black Sabbath-style riffing.

If we play the D chord from the fifth string, we get a second inversion with the 5th (A) in the bass.

A useful root triad begins on the fourth string. This one is ideal for situations where we want to avoid playing in the same range as the bass player, but still want to play a full major triad. Jimi Hendrix used this shape a lot, sometimes adding his thumb over the neck to play an additional low root note on the sixth string.

The third string yields a warm sounding, friendly first inversion with the third (F#) as the lowest note. This voicing is often used in Motown songs and also shows up throughout pop music.

D Major (E shape) · D Major (E shape) · D Major (E shape) · D Major (E shape) · D Major (E shape)

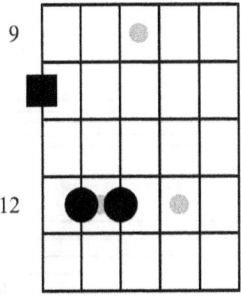

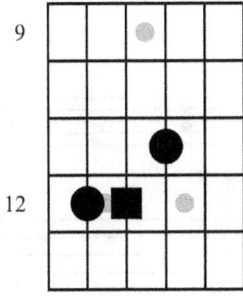

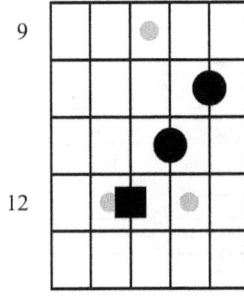

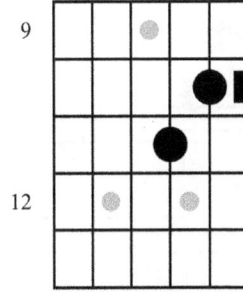

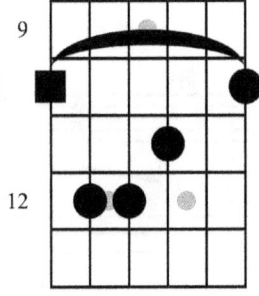

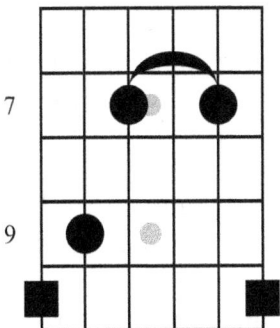

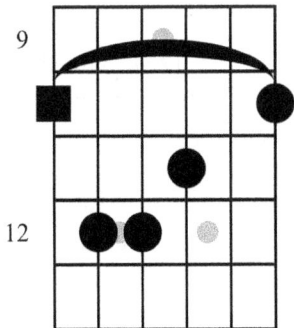

Example 1k:

D5   D/A   D   D/F#   D

Combining CAGED G and E Shapes

As we did with the C and A shapes, we can combine CAGED G and E shapes and add some embellishments. Take a moment to commit to memory how the G shape and E shape are located next to each other on the fretboard. Get used to playing fragments of each chord shape and experiment by jumping between them.

D Major (G shape) · D Major (E shape)

Example 1l:

Example 1m:

CAGED D Shape: power chord and inversions

The lower register of the CAGED D shape is less commonly used, but it is useful to help you visualize the full range of the D chord in its movable position.

If we fill in the missing notes and play the D shape on the bottom three strings, we form a first inversion with the 3rd (F#) in the bass. This is the same Hendrix/Mayer style inversion you played in the CAGED G shape, transported to a lower string set.

Playing from the fifth string we get an inverted power chord with the 5th (A) in the bass.

If we begin playing from the fourth string, we get another power chord (D5), with the fourth finger moving up a fret to play an octave of the root on the second string. This chord voicing harkens back to 1980's heavy rock, and you'll often find it in songs by bands such as Dokken, Mötley Crüe and Ozzy Osbourne.

Beginning the D chord on the third string yields a second inversion D triad with the 5th (A) in the bass. This three-string shape is much easier to move up/down the neck than playing the full CAGED D shape, which is why it's so important to be able to visualize these inversions as part of the larger shape. This movable D triad has a jangly, open sound, often heard in songs by bands such as The Who, The Byrds and Tom Petty. If you like this sound, you may need a Rickenbacker!

D Major
(D shape)   D Major
(D shape)   D Major
(D shape)   D Major
(D shape)   D Major
(D shape)

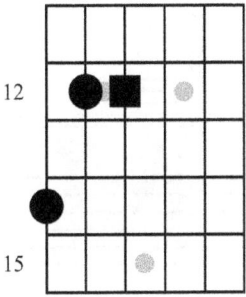

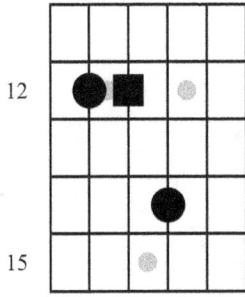

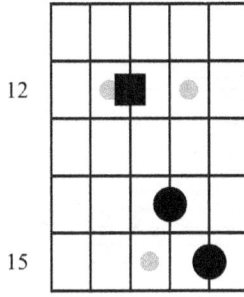

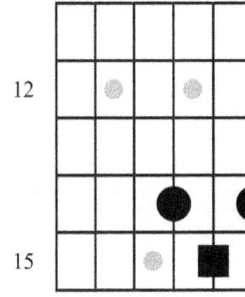

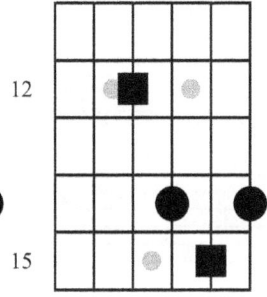

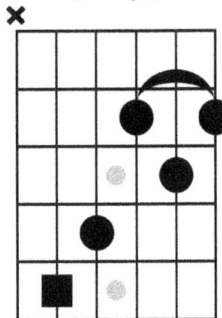

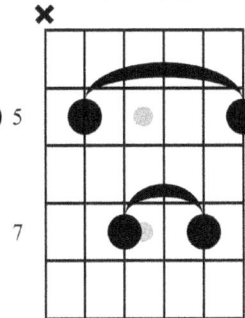

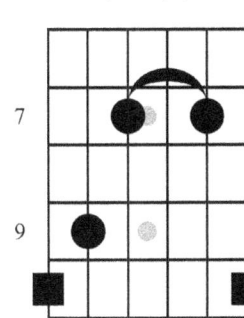

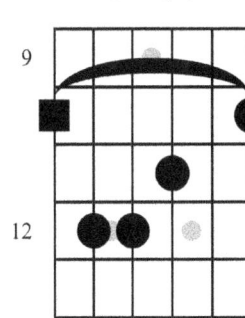

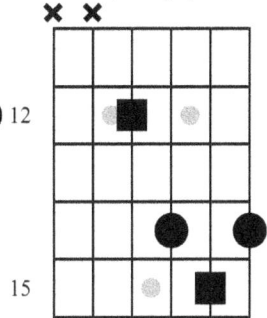

Example 1n:

D/F♯   D5/A   D5   D/A   D

Combining CAGED D major shapes

The real power of the CAGED system can be seen when we combine all five shapes. If you diligently practiced breaking each chord down into three-string voicings, I'm sure you can see that, with all five shapes in action, you now have multiple voicings for D major covering a huge range of the fretboard.

As we progress through the book, you'll get to practice combining shapes much more, but for now, here are two examples of playing a D major chord that combine all five CAGED shapes and add some embellishments.

D Major
(C shape)   D Major
(A shape)   D Major
(G shape)   D Major
(E shape)   D Major
(D shape)

Example 1o:

Example 1p:

In the next chapter, you'll take your shape visualization skills a step further and learn how to transfer this knowledge to a different key.

Chapter Two: CAGED Major Chords in a Different Key

A Major chord – CAGED G Shape: root triad and inversions

Since the majority of songs contain more chords than just D major, let's ensure you can find another major chord all over the neck using the CAGED system.

CAGED chord shapes always ascend the neck in the same order (C then A then G, etc). However, depending on what chord we want to play, the C shape won't always be the lowest possible voicing.

Take an A major chord, for example. The lowest position in which we can play it is the open position (the A shape). So, the next shape in the system will be the G shape, and so on. When you practice playing CAGED shapes with any chord, always think about what shape will give you the lowest position on the neck as your starting point.

You know the A open chord, so let's use the CAGED G shape to play A major, then play the three-string voicings (root triad and first/second inversions) that are found inside it, just like we did for D major.

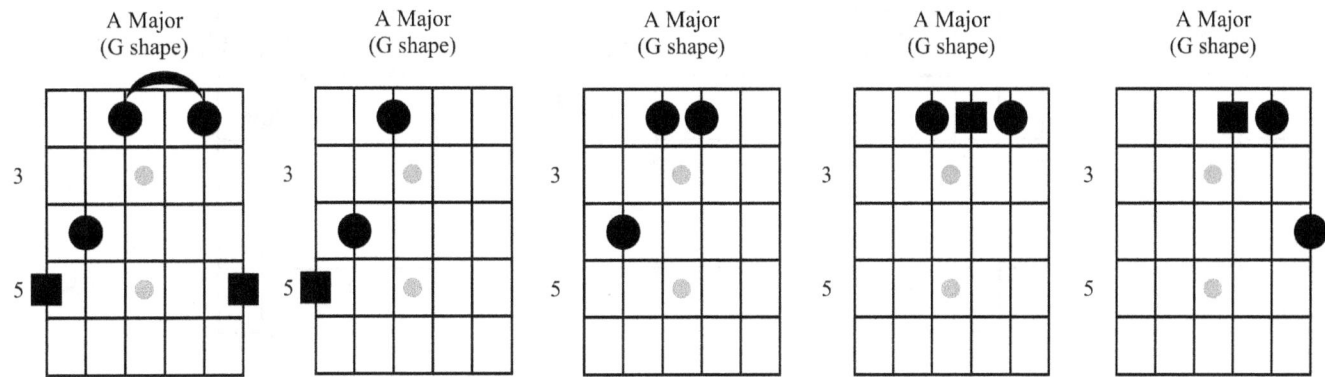

| A Major (G shape) | A Major (G shape) | A Major (G shape) | A Major (G shape) | A Major (G shape) |

Example 2a:

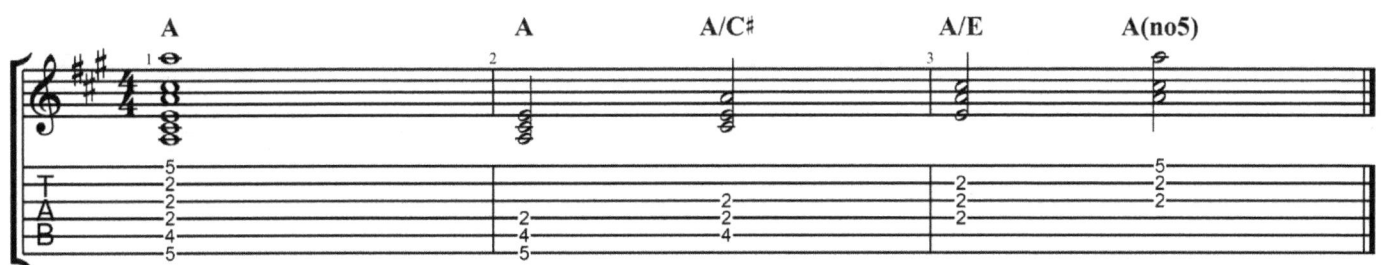

Your Turn! Find the next two CAGED shapes for A Major

I always encourage my students to visualize the fretboard and not to rely solely on charts/TAB to tell them what to play. So, using the knowledge you've gained, locate the next two CAGED shapes for A major. Go through this process with each one:

First, play the full CAGED chord shape, then find and play the three-string voicings located inside it. Refer back to the CAGED D chord shapes to help you.

Hint: Remember, the word C-A-G-E-D gives you the *order* of the shapes and it's the same every time. We just played the G shape, so the E shape will be next, then the D. Don't worry if you find this a struggle at the moment, the answer shall be revealed in a second.

If you managed to locate/play the E and D shapes successfully, the next one is the C shape, which I'll spell out for you.

A Major chord – CAGED C Shape: root triad and inversions

Here's the CAGED C shape for A major, with its root note on the 12th fret. As before, play the full shape, then the smaller three-string voicings. Practice moving between them as before.

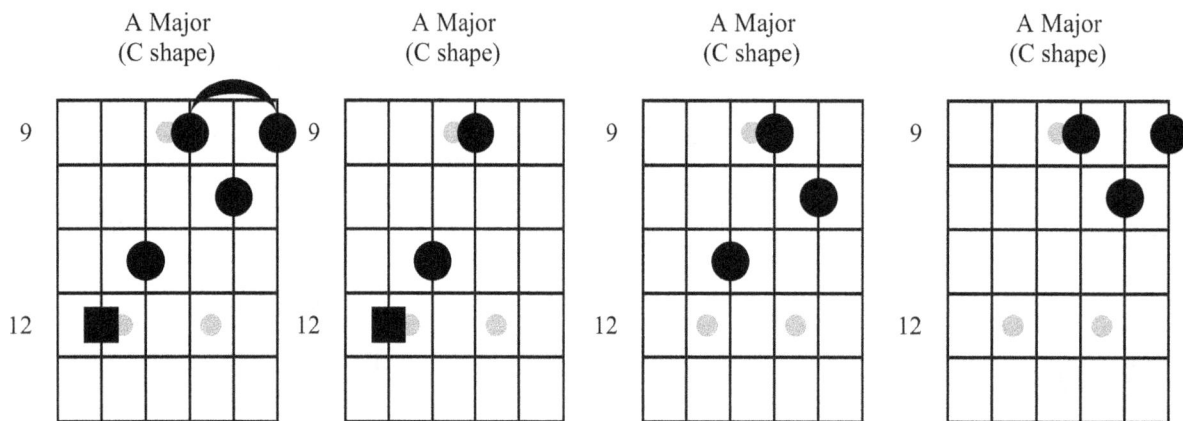

Example 2b:

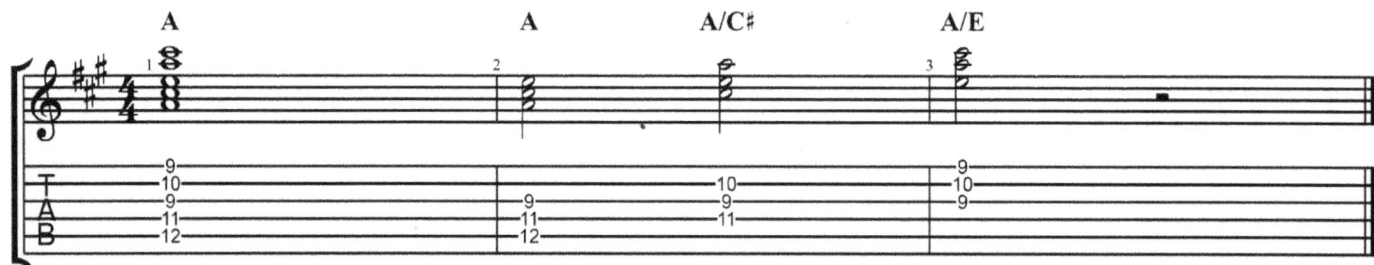

A Major chord – CAGED A Shape: power chord, root triad and inversions

The last CAGED shape for A major is the open A shape, barred with its root note on the fifth string, 12th fret. Remember, the A shape intersects with the G shape, which is a helpful visual reference point.

A Major
(A shape)

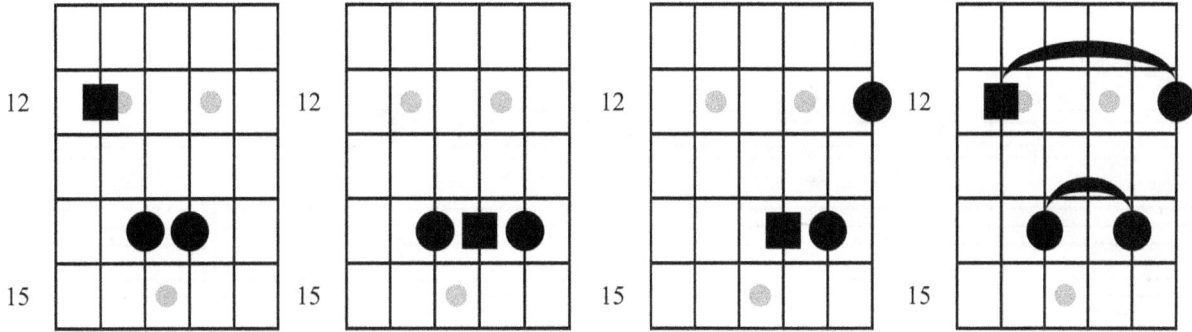

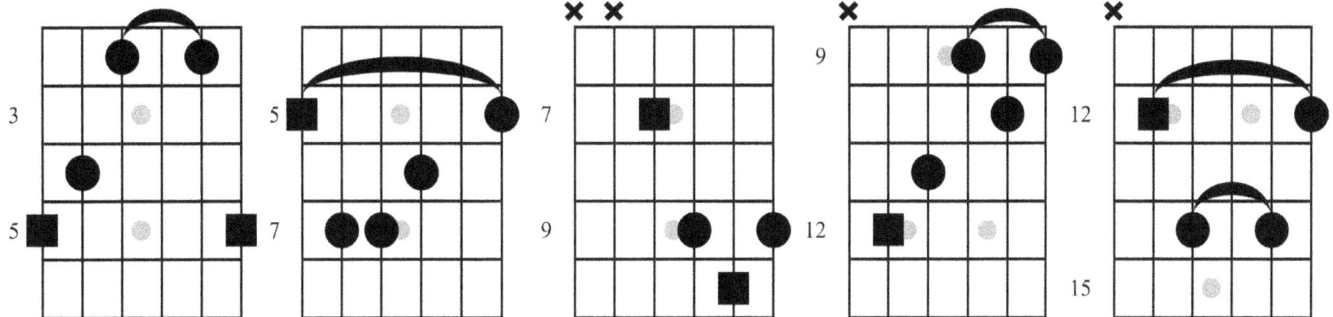

A Major
(A shape)

A Major
(A shape)

A Major
(A shape)

Example 2c:

A5   A/E   A   A

A Major chord: five CAGED shapes

Finally, here are all five CAGED shapes for A major. In Example 2d, first play an open A major chord, then play the CAGED shapes beginning with the G shape. We've jumped into the system at A, so are following the pattern A-G-E-D-C-A. You can see that the word CAGED just keeps starting over until we run out of fretboard.

For practice, play through the shapes in a methodical manner, first sounding the full chord shape, then playing each of the three-note voicings inside.

A Major
(G shape)

A Major
(E shape)

A Major
(D shape)

A Major
(C shape)

A Major
(A shape)

Example 2d:

Combining CAGED A major shapes

To end this chapter, here's a musical way of playing A major combining all five CAGED shapes, adding some embellishments.

Example 2e:

Now you understand how to work with the CAGED system, test yourself with another chord. How about a Bb major?

Q: where is the lowest position on the neck you can play it and with what shape?

A: it's with the root note on the fifth string, 1st fret, and using the A shape.

Now work through the rest of the CAGED shapes to ascend the neck until you run out of fretboard.

Chapter Three: Applying CAGED Major Chords

Combining two major chords

Now that you have a good understanding of major CAGED forms, and can visualize the small voicings within the larger shapes, let's focus on getting musical. We'll begin by moving between C major and G major chords – a very common chord combination – in different places on the neck.

In this short chapter, we'll identify the best shapes to use to keep the chord voicings closely connected, then in Chapter Four we'll explore adding embellishments around these shapes. After that, we'll add in a third chord to play a popular chord progression.

C to G played on the first, second and third strings using CAGED A and E shapes

Let's being with the 3rd position A shape for C major. Located right next to it is a G major chord using the CAGED E shape. I'm only showing you chord fragments here, arranged on the top three strings, but I want you to play and visualize the larger CAGED shapes.

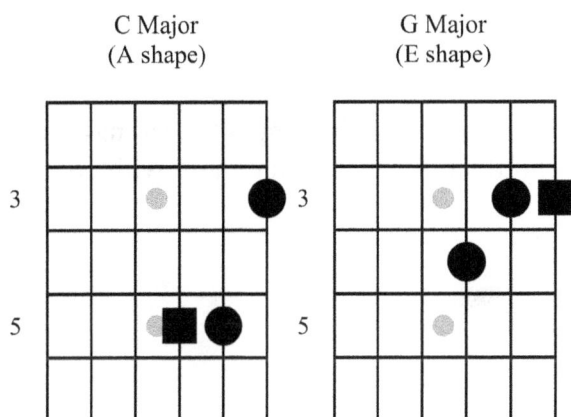

C Major (A shape)   G Major (E shape)

When playing these smaller voicings, notice the half step movement of the note C to B on the third string, as the root of the C chord moves to the 3rd of the G chord (B). It gives a musically pleasing way to hear the transition between the two chords.

Example 3a:

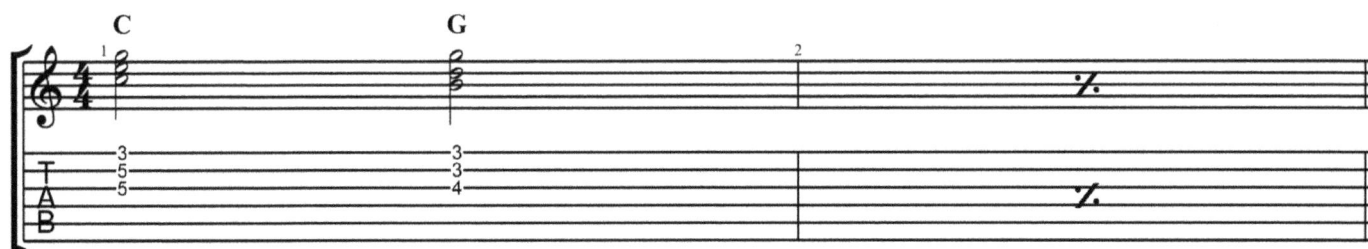

For the rest of this chapter, we're going to move the C major chord through the CAGED shapes in order, with the G major chord following behind in its own sequence. I.e. we began with the A shape for C major, so the next CAGED shape will be G. And we began with the E shape for G major, so the next shape will be D, and so on.

C to G played on the second, third and fourth strings using CAGED G and D shapes

C Major
(G shape)

G Major
(D shape)

Notice in the second measure below that the bass note of the C chord on the sixth string, 8th fret, moves to the 3rd (B) of the G chord on the 7th. Without the B note, the G chord would be a power chord with no 3rd. Adding it creates a nice descending bass movement.

Example 3b:

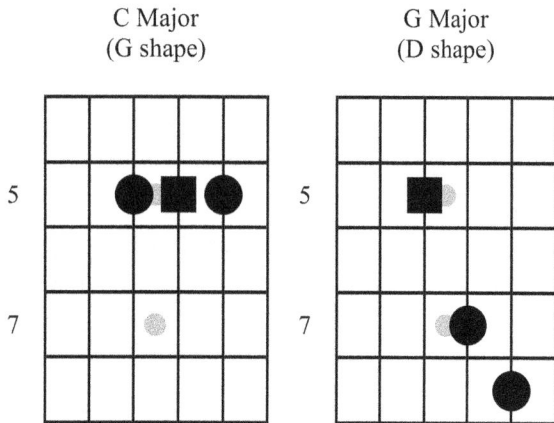

C to G played on the second, third and fourth strings using CAGED E and C shapes

Now let's repeat the process with the CAGED E and C shapes.

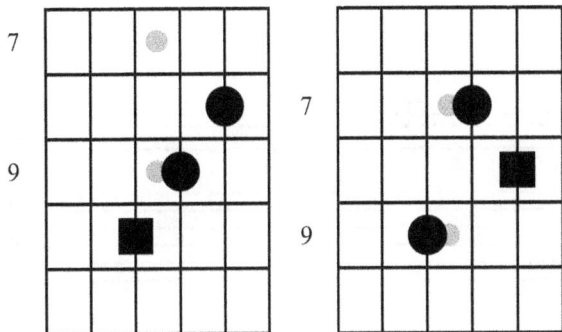

C Major
(E shape)

G Major
(C shape)

The movement from the note C to B, found in the previous examples, now occurs on the fourth string.

Example 3c:

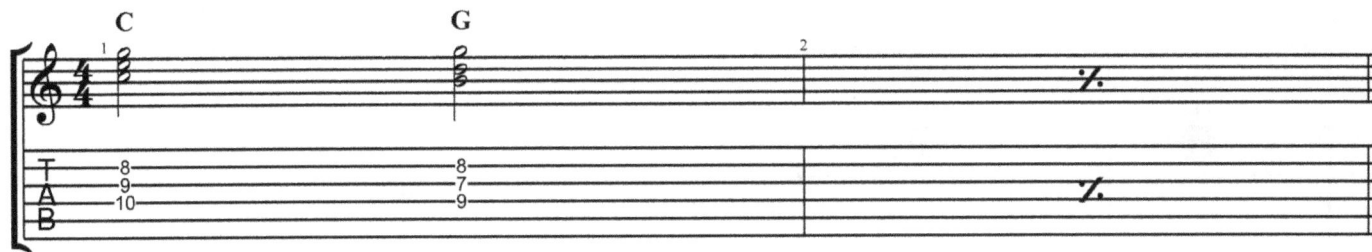

C to G played on the second, third and fourth strings using CAGED D and A shapes

Next, we play C to G using the CAGED D and A shapes. Remember to visualize the larger CAGED shapes and actually play them before playing the smaller voicings.

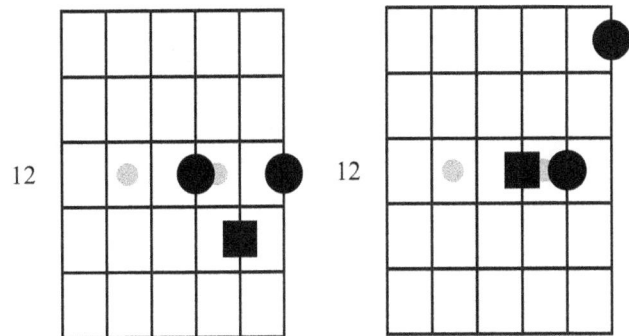

C Major
(D shape)

G Major
(A shape)

The movement from C to B now happens on the second string.

Example 3d:

C to G played on the third, fourth and fifth strings using CAGED C and G shapes

Complete the pattern by playing the C to G cadence with CAGED C and G shapes.

The movement from C to B is now on the fifth string.

Example 3e:

Previously, if you saw the chord change C to G on a chart, the chances are you'd have reached for familiar block chord shapes to play it. But now you know five different ways to play it, in zones covering the full range of the neck. Plus, you can play it using economical, three-note shapes that will fit into any musical context. Now, let's take things a step further and embellish those chord changes.

Chapter Four: Adding Embellishments to CAGED Major Chords

One of the most useful aspects of applying the CAGED system in the way we're doing here, is that playing smaller chord fragments makes it much easier to add embellishments around them. Whether your bag is Motown, Hendrix-inspired blues-rock, spicy Chili Peppers funk, or John Mayer-style pop and beyond, the methods used to add embellishments follow a recurring theme. Let's examine some of them!

Suspended chords

Let's look again at the way we played C to G on the top three strings using CAGED A and E shapes. We can embellish these voicings by moving our fourth/first fingers to add notes located around the chord shapes.

For example, hold down the C major A shape as normal, then use the fourth finger to add a note on the second string, 6th fret. This creates a Csus4 sound.

Move the first finger to fret the top two strings at the 3rd fret, while the third finger remains on the third string, 5th fret, and we create a Csus2 sound.

We can do a similar thing with the G chord.

Put these ideas together and we can use the suspended chord sounds to create a simple, yet melodic rhythm part.

C Major
(A shape)

G Major
(E shape)

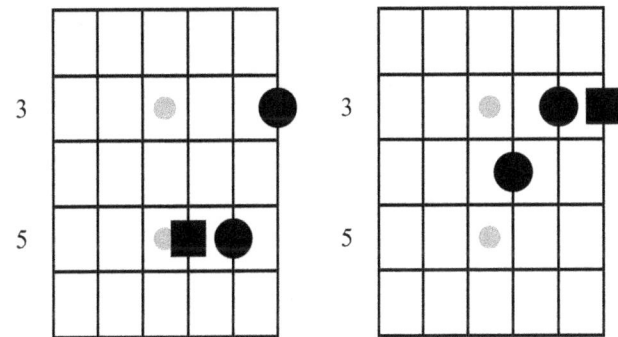

Example 4a:

Pentatonic fills

If we revisit C to G played on the second, third and fourth strings using CAGED G and D shapes, we can add some single-note fills using the notes of the C Major Pentatonic scale (C D E G A).

Here's a reminder of the shapes:

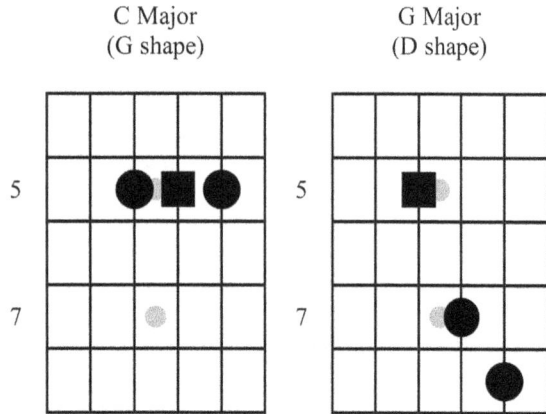

C Major
(G shape)

G Major
(D shape)

And here is the C Major Pentatonic scale in this zone of the neck:

C Major Pentatonic (CAGED G Shape)

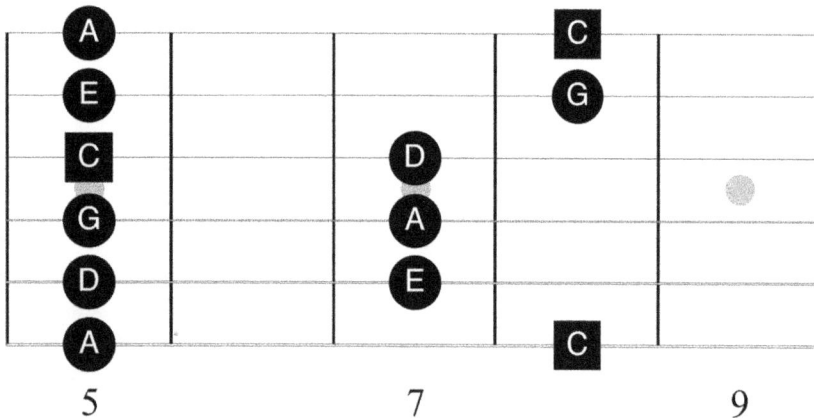

Example 4b shows how to combine these stripped-back chord voicings with the major pentatonic scale to create a cool, bluesy John Mayer-style riff.

Example 4b:

Sliding 4th's

If we revisit C to G played on the second, third and fourth strings using CAGED E and C shapes, we can extract some 4th's played as double-stops for a different musical effect. A double-stop is just a way of describing two notes played simultaneously on adjacent strings.

You can view this idea as C Major Pentatonic based, but this time arranged around the CAGED E shape. Sliding into and out of the double-stops adds some fluidity to the sound.

C Major
(E shape)

G Major
(C shape)

C Major Pentatonic (CAGED E Shape)

Example 4c:

3rd's as double-stops

If we revisit C to G played on the first, second and third strings using CAGED A and E shapes, we can incorporate some 3rd intervals played as double-stops. This time the embellishment notes come from the full C Major scale (C D E F G A B). Thirds are a tried and tested way to create nice melodic parts that connect together the chords.

C Major
(A shape)

G Major
(E shape)

As an exercise (there is no audio for this), play through the C Major scale harmonized into 3rds and internalize the sound.

C Major scale in 3rd's as double-stops

Now hear how this idea can be converted into a melodic phrase with a soulful vibe, which incorporates our CAGED voicings.

Example 4d:

Popular song form: the I–V–IV sequence

So far we've worked on the transition between C and G major chords. Now let's add a third chord (F) to create a popular chord progression.

The chord movement C to G to F is known as the I–V–IV progression. The Roman numerals refer to the position of each chord in the harmonized C Major scale. Let me briefly explain this, as the idea will crop up more as we progress.

The C Major scale contains the notes C D E F G A B.

If we take the first note of the scale, then stack notes in 3rd intervals on top of it, we form a chord. A 3rd interval means every other note, i.e. C, then E, then G. The three notes C E G form the chord C major.

Moving to the second note in the scale, we take the D note, then stack 3rds on top of it. The result is D, F and A, which forms a D minor chord.

Stacking notes in 3rds to create chords is called *harmonizing* the scale. This is the result if we harmonize the whole scale:

C major – D minor – E minor – F major – G major – A minor – B diminished

These seven chords are each allocated a Roman numeral – an upper case numeral if it's a major type chord or a lower case numeral if it's a minor chord. Describing the harmonized scale in Roman numerals we get:

I (C major), ii (D minor), iii (E minor), IV (F major), V (G major), vi (A minor), vii (B diminished)

Why all the Roman numerals, you may well ask!

Musicians use this numbering system as a quick, shorthand way of describing a chord progression in any key. Rather than say, "We're going to play this chord, then that chord…" etc., it's easier to say, "It's a I-V-IV in the key of C." That statement describes both the type of each chord, and the order in which they appear.

Don't worry if this sounds a bit baffling for now. Later, as we continue to refer to chord progressions, you'll get the idea.

Now, let's apply what we've learned so far and play these chords in several areas of the neck, as well as adding some embellishments.

Playing C - G - F on the second, third and fourth strings using CAGED E, C and A shapes

In bar one, a D note on the third string 7th fret is added below the CAGED E shape. It's the suspended 2nd of the chord and works nicely with the 3rd (E) of the chord on the 9th fret.

The notes that follow this phrase walk smoothly into the G chord, with its B note in the bass, derived from the CAGED C shape.

The F chord begins as a CAGED A shape, then morphs into the G shape as we slide up the 3rd (A) and play the root and 5th (F and C).

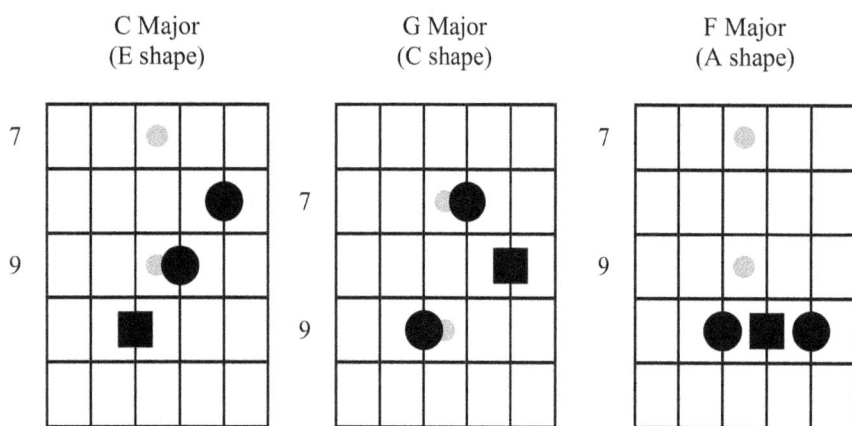

C Major
(E shape)

G Major
(C shape)

F Major
(A shape)

Example 4e:

Playing C - G - F on the first, second and third strings using CAGED G, D and C shapes

By utilizing 3rd's played as double-stops we can create a melody that connects the chords. The 3rd's are constructed from the C Major scale. Play through them as an exercise (there is no audio for this), to get the sound in your head.

C Major in 3rd's as double-stops

Here are the CAGED shapes for this zone of the neck:

C Major
(G shape)

G Major
(D shape)

F Major
(C shape)

Walking up from the C chord to the G chord then back to the F chord with 3rds adds some melodic interest. Turning the F chord into a suspended 2nd (with the note G), yields a less resolved sound that becomes resolved when the C chord starts the progression over again. These embellishments bring a lot to a simple three-chord progression!

Example 4f:

There are numerous ways we could connect these three chords, adding embellishments, so take some time to experiment with them and try inventing your own. In the next chapter we're going to start the process again, this time with minor chords.

Chapter Five: Identifying CAGED Minor Chords

Now we shift our attention to locating and playing minor chords using the CAGED system. As with major chords, each open chord shape (C minor, A minor, G minor, E minor and D minor) represents a moveable chord form.

CAGED C minor shape

The first minor chord shape in the CAGED system is the Cm shape. When we play Cm in the open position, the third string is played open. To create a moveable version of this shape, we move up the neck and use our fourth finger to play the root note on the fifth string.

To play an Em chord using the C shape, for example, play the notes on the fourth, third and second strings with the second, first and third fingers respectively, and stretch the fourth finger over to play the root note (E) at the 7th fret.

Don't worry if this chord voicing feels a little awkward to play. We know that the real magic of this shape lies in the triad played on the second, third and fourth strings. Take a moment to visualize how the Cm shape has been transformed into an Em chord.

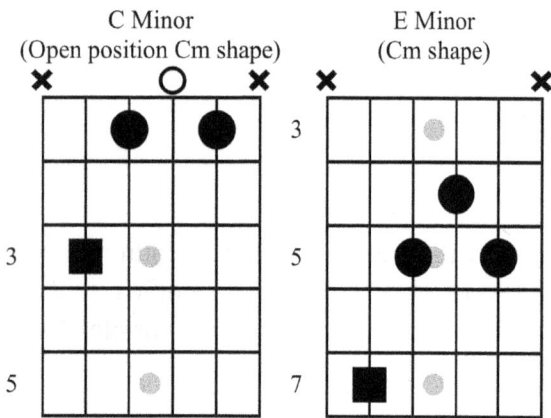

C Minor
(Open position Cm shape)

E Minor
(Cm shape)

Example 5a:

CAGED A minor shape

The second minor chord shape in the CAGED system is the Am shape.

Let's play an Em chord using this shape.

When we play an Am chord in the open position, the first and fifth strings are played open. Therefore, to make the shape moveable, our first finger becomes a barre, and the rest of the notes are played with the second, third and fourth fingers.

To play an Em chord using the Am shape, the first finger barres the 7th fret, beginning from the root note (E) on the fifth string.

You're probably familiar with this shape as it is a widely used minor barre chord. Just be sure to visualize how the *open Am chord shape* has been moved up the neck to play this Em chord.

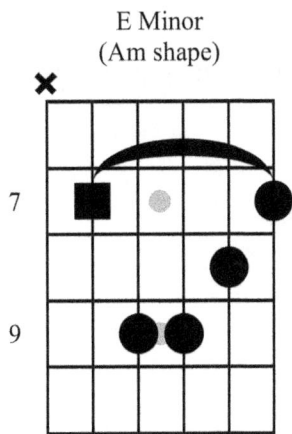

E Minor
(Am shape)

Example 5b:

CAGED G minor shape

The third chord shape is the Gm shape.

This one is unusual as it appears awkward to play and has several variations. Don't worry too much about this, however, the most important thing at this stage is to be able to visualize the shape.

Here's how we can play an Em chord using this shape.

One way is to fret the sixth string root (E) with the third finger, then play the note G on the fifth string with the second finger. This way allows your first finger to make a barre across the third and fourth strings. You can play the first and second strings using your fourth finger – if you can reach!

As an alternative, fret the sixth string root (E) with the fourth finger, play the note G on the fifth string with the second finger, then use the first finger for the third/fourth strings barre. This is a common variation where we omit the first and second strings.

Yet another alternative has the fourth finger barred across the first, second and third strings.

Don't stress if you can't get this chord to sound completely clean using any of these variations – just look at the way the Gm shape has been used to play an Em chord.

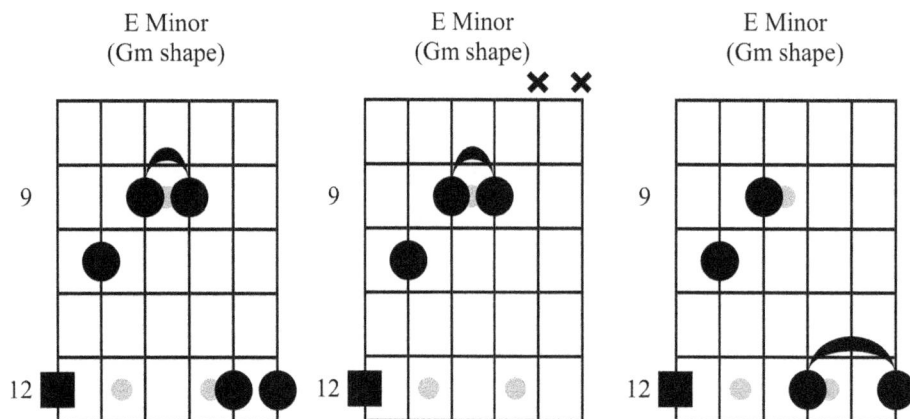

Example 5c:

CAGED E minor shape

The fourth CAGED shape is one I'm sure you have played before – the Em shape.

To make the Em shape moveable, the first finger is used to barre all the strings. To play an Em chord, the E root note is located at the 12th fret on the sixth string, so we barre across the strings at the 12th. Take a moment and see that you're playing an open Em chord shape in your familiar barre chord.

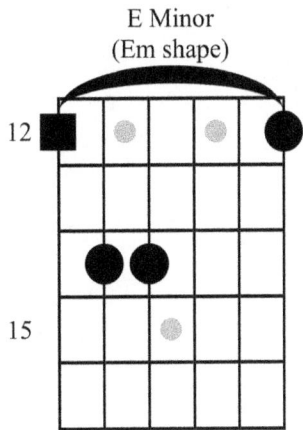

E Minor
(Em shape)

Example 5d:

CAGED D minor shape

The fifth and final CAGED minor shape is the Dm shape.

We'll play an Em chord using the Dm shape.

To fret the part of the shape that looks like an open Dm chord, use your second, fourth and third fingers on the third, second and first strings respectively. When we play an open Dm chord, the fourth string is played open, but in the moveable shape your first finger will play the root note on the fourth string.

Take a moment to visualize the shape and see how this shape resembles an open Dm chord.

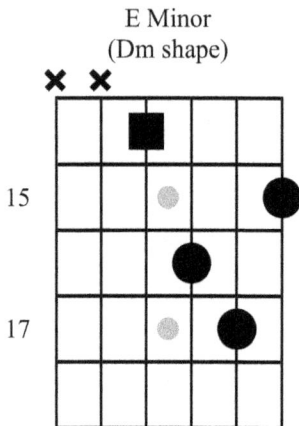

E Minor
(Dm shape)

Example 5e:

Finding inversions within the shapes

So far, we've played an Em chord in five positions on the fretboard and covered a wide range of the neck using the minor CAGED shapes. Next, we're going to investigate the musical gems hiding in plain sight within these minor CAGED shapes, just as we did with the major shapes.

CAGED Cm shape: root triad and inversions

Let's return to the CAGED Cm shape and play an Em chord, this time breaking it down into smaller shapes across groups of three strings. Note that these smaller shapes are all found inside the larger shape.

In the first three-string voicing we have the root note (E) on the fifth string 7th fret, the 3rd (G) of the chord on the fourth string, and the 5th (B) on the third string. This gives us a closed voice Em triad – like playing an arpeggio.

The most useful voicing of this chord is the first inversion (the middle shape in the diagram below), with the 3rd as the lowest note. It's ideal for minor blues rhythm applications and you can slide into it from above or below to add emotion.

Although doing so strays into Dm shape territory, we can also add a G note on the first string, 3rd fret to complete a second inversion shape on the top three strings.

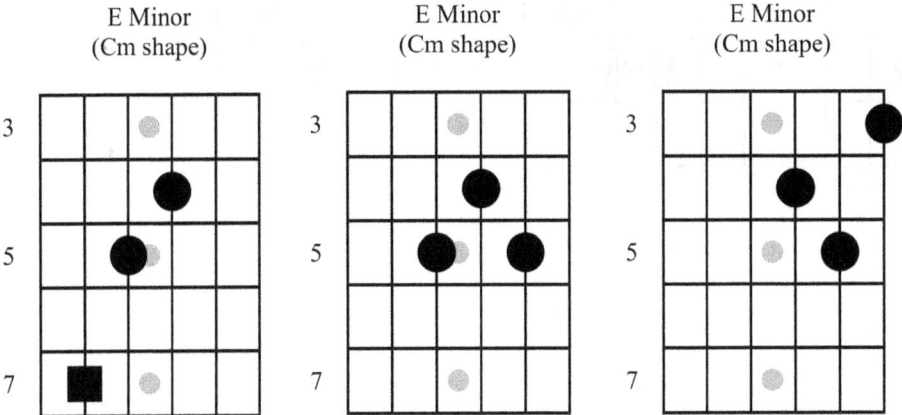

E Minor
(Cm shape)

E Minor
(Cm shape)

E Minor
(Cm shape)

Example 5f:

CAGED Am shape: power chords, inversion, root triad

Playing an Em chord using the CAGED Am shape, the notes on the sixth, fifth and fourth strings form an inverted power chord that has no 3rd. It's inverted because the lowest note is the 5th rather than the root. This is a handy voicing for simulating Drop-D style heavy riffing without having to detune your sixth string.

In the next three-note grouping we get a traditional power chord with an E root note.

A second inversion follows with the notes B, E and G. This is a nice visual reminder that we are inside the CAGED Am shape. If you fret this the same way you'd play an open Am chord (with the second, third and first fingers), then the fourth finger is free to add embellishments – such as grabbing the A note on the second string, 10th fret, for an Esus4 sound.

The root triad is played on the top three strings, spelled E, G, B and is very a useful voicing. Think of every funk song you've ever heard or slide it up to Gm (with the root note G at the 12th fret) and you've got the start of a Cream classic!

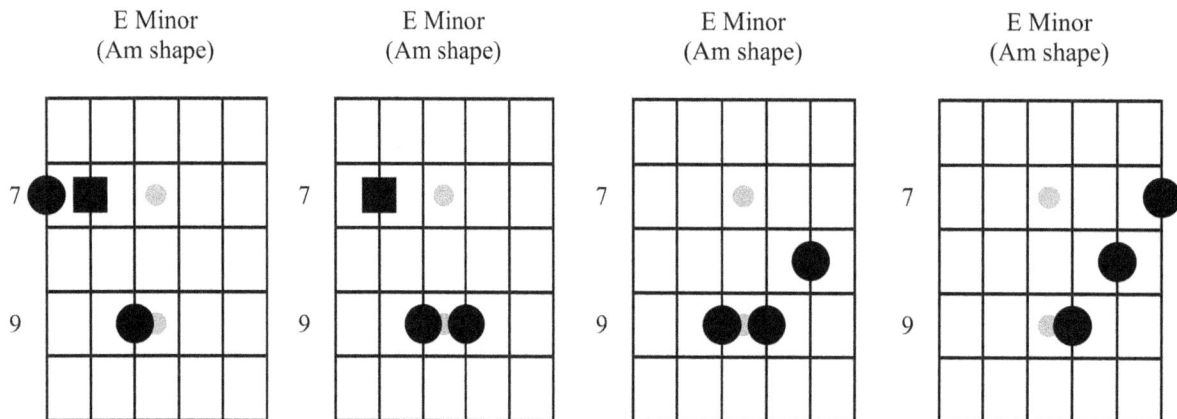

E Minor (Am shape)	E Minor (Am shape)	E Minor (Am shape)	E Minor (Am shape)

Example 5g:

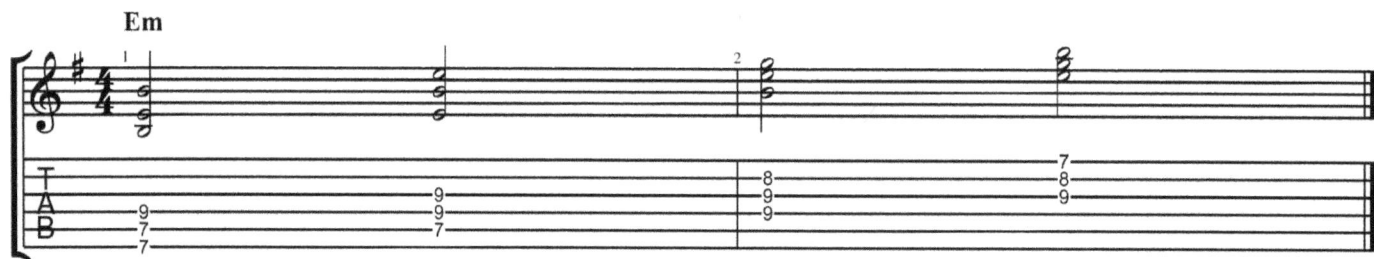

Combining CAGED Cm and Am shapes

Now that we've broken apart the Cm and Am shapes, here are two examples that show how to play an Em chord combining the two shapes and adding some embellishments. We'll delve into where these embellishments come from in more detail later on. For now, just look at how the Cm and Am shapes are located next to each other on the fretboard. Get used to playing fragments of each chord shape and combining them.

E Minor
(Cm shape)

E Minor
(Am shape)

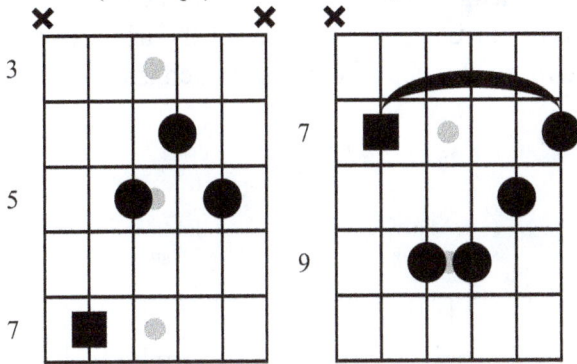

Example 5h1:

Example 5h2:

CAGED Gm shape: root triad, inversion and power chord)

Now let's break apart the Gm shape of an Em chord. The three-note grouping on the bottom three strings spells a closed voice E minor triad, with the root note on the sixth string, the 3rd (G) on the fifth string, and the 5th (B) on the fourth string.

Playing the next three-string group from the fifth string, yields a first inversion. An inverted power chord shows up next, with the fifth (B) played on the fourth and second strings, and the root note (E) on the third string. You can play another power chord on the top three strings, or barre across all three for the triad, which connects to the Em shape. Being aware of these options gives you more choices of voicing, which is especially useful if you're playing different genres of music.

E Minor (Gm shape)   E Minor (Gm shape)   E Minor (Gm shape)   E Minor (Gm shape)   E Minor (Gm shape)

Example 5i:

CAGED Em shape: power chord, inversions, root triad)

Playing the Em shape from its root on the sixth string gives us an E power chord as it has no 3rd, just the notes E, B, E, but you already knew that!

Next a second inversion beginning with the note B on the fifth string sits inside the main Em voicing.

The root triad in this shape (with the root note on the fourth string) is extremely useful, as it has the full sound of the minor chord but doesn't get in the way of a bass or keys player. This voicing also allows for embellishments in the Jimi/S.R.V. tradition.

Finally, the first inversion played on the top three strings is another useful voicing which has been applied in everything from funk to rock, and also in pop songs, such as *Roxanne* by The Police.

E Minor
(Em shape)   E Minor
(Em shape)   E Minor
(Em shape)   E Minor
(Em shape)

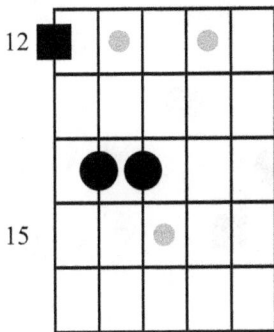

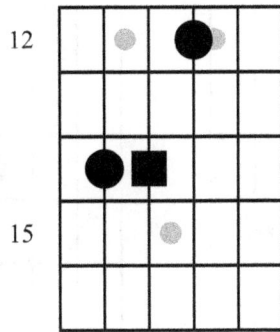

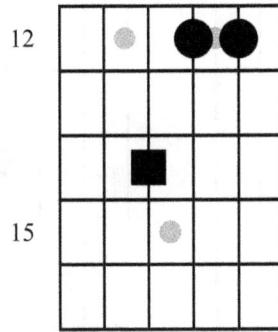

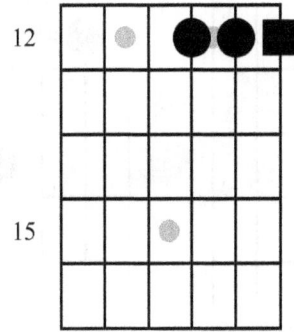

Example 5j:

CAGED Dm shape: inversion, power chords, root triad

The lower register of the CAGED Dm shape is less commonly used because it can sound quite dense, but is nonetheless useful to help us visualize the full range of the moveable Dm chord shape. The first three-string group played from the sixth string gives us a first inversion with the 3rd (G) in the bass.

On the fifth string we get an inverted power chord with the 5th (A) in the bass.

If we begin from the fourth string we get another power chord (D5) with the fourth finger moving up a fret to play an octave of the root on the second string.

The second inversion with the fifth (B) played on the third string has all the melodic goodness of the open Dm chord but without the open string, so this is a very useful chord form. We don't need no education, but perhaps a little helps? See what I did there?

E Minor (Dm shape)   E Minor (Dm shape)   E Minor (Dm shape)   E Minor (Dm shape)

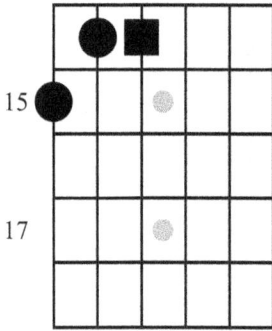

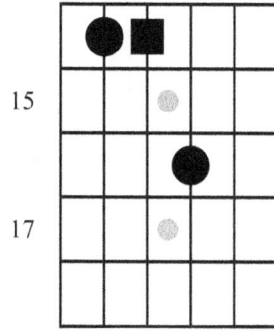

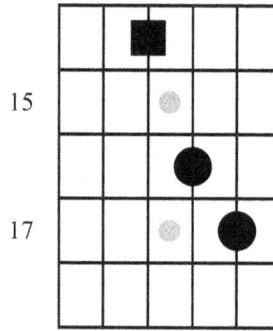

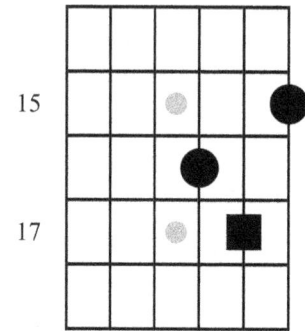

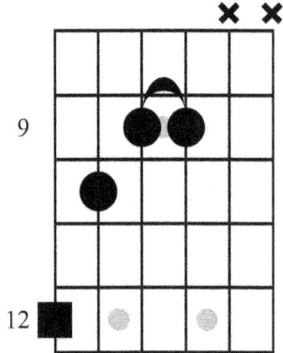

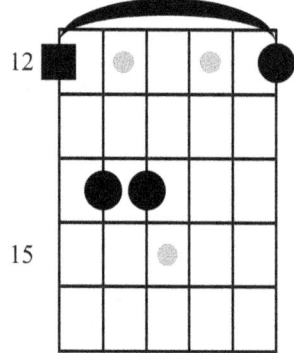

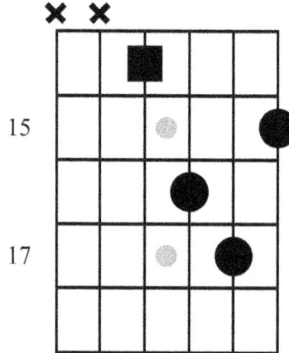

Example 5k:

Em

Combining CAGED Gm, Em and Dm Shapes

Here are two examples playing an Em chord that combine Gm, Em and Dm shapes, adding some embellishments.

E Minor (Gm shape)   E Minor (Em shape)   E Minor (Dm shape)

First, a way of combining shape fragments to create something much more interesting than chugging on a single Em shape.

Example 5l1:

And a bluesy line that makes use of the three-string group from the fifth string.

Example 5l2:

Chapter Six: CAGED Minor Chords in a Different Key

Just as we did for the major CAGED shapes, let's ensure you can transfer this knowledge and find another minor chord all over the neck using the CAGED system.

Remember, just like the major shapes, CAGED minor chord shapes always ascend the neck in the *same* order, spelling the word CAGED. However, depending on what chord you want to play, the Cm shape won't necessarily be the lowest and therefore the starting point.

This time we'll play a Bm chord. It means that the CAGED Am shape is the lowest available and our starting point in the system.

Play the full Am CAGED shape for Bm, then the three-string group voicings that sit inside it. The root triad played on the first, second and third strings is a particularly useful funky voicing you'll have heard before.

B minor chord: CAGED Am shape (root triad, power chord & inversions)

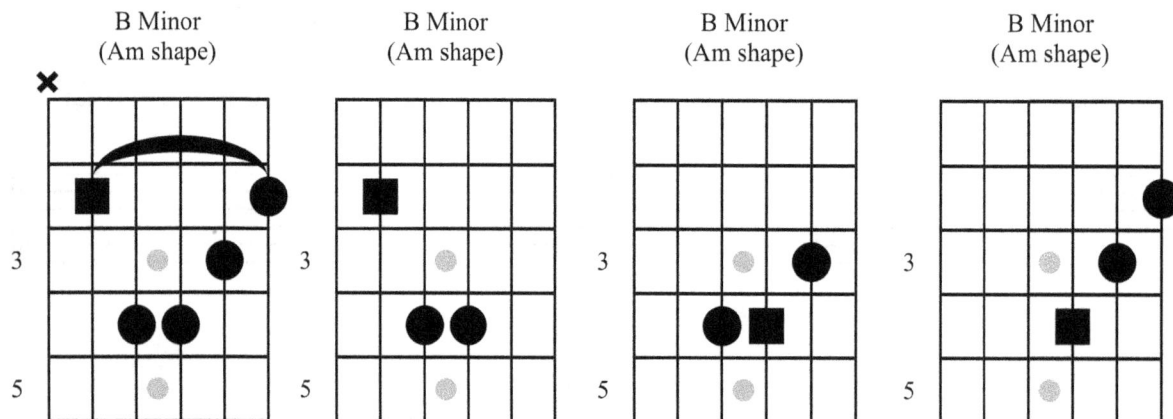

Example 6a:

B minor chord – CAGED Gm shape: root triad, power chord and inversions

Here's a Bm chord played using the CAGED Gm shape, broken into three-note voicings. The root triad is followed by a first inversion and an inverted power chord. The first inversion played on the first, second and third strings pivots between CAGED Gm and Em shapes.

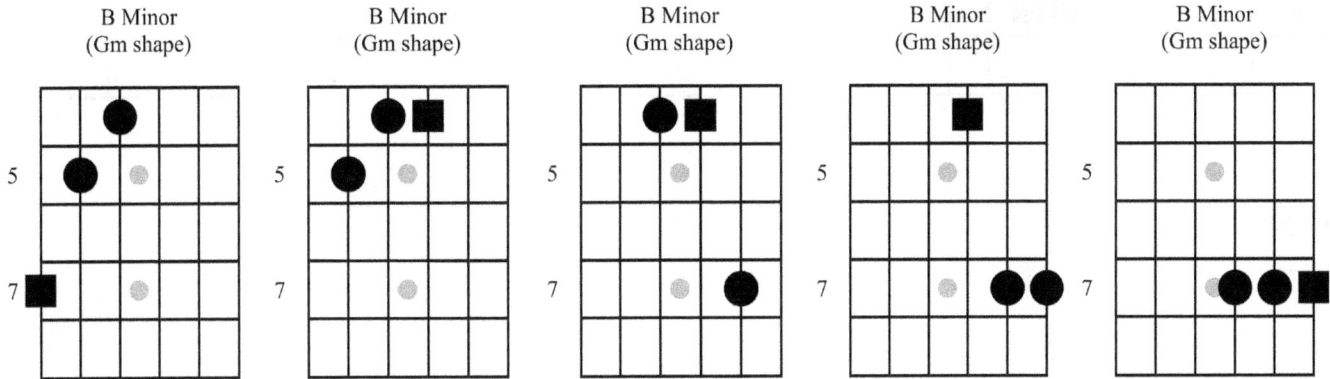

Example 6b:

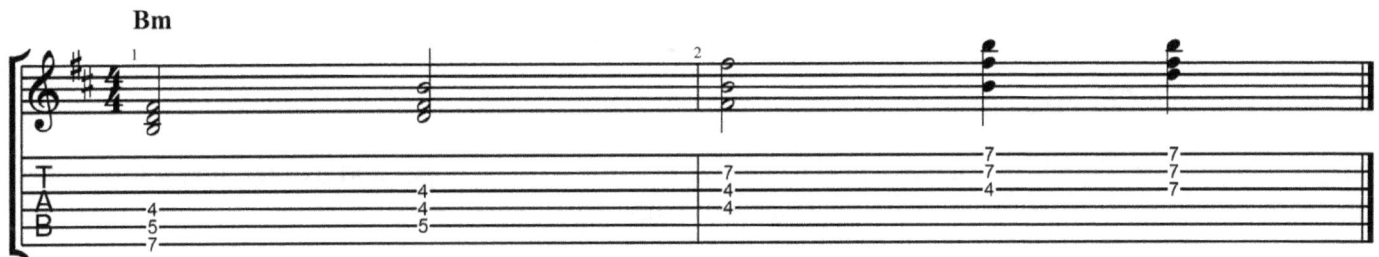

Your turn! Find the next two CAGED shapes for B Minor

As part of your quest to visualize chord shapes on the fretboard, work out the next two CAGED shapes for Bm. For each shape, play the full CAGED chord shape then find the three-string voicings inside it.

If you need to, look back at the CAGED Em chords to help you visualize the shapes. Don't stress if you can't find them, the answer will be revealed in a moment.

Once you've found them, continue with the Bm chord played using the CAGED Cm shape.

B minor chord – CAGED Cm shape: root triad and inversions

As mentioned previously, a useful voicing found within this shape is the first inversion. In this key, the 3rd (D) is played on the 12th fret of the fourth string with the second finger. A second inversion with the 5th (F#) as the lowest note, in this position pivots between CAGED Cm and Dm shapes – another handy visual.

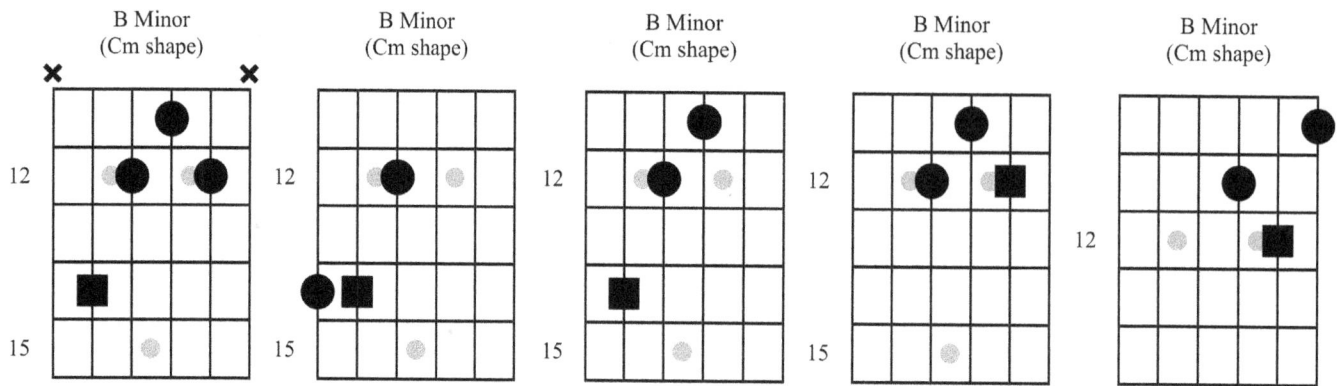

B Minor (Cm shape) — B Minor (Cm shape) — B Minor (Cm shape) — B Minor (Cm shape) — B Minor (Cm shape)

Example 6c:

Bm

B minor chord: 5 CAGED shapes

Now you should be able to play a Bm chord using five minor CAGED shapes and extract the root triad, first inversion and second inversion chord voicings in each shape.

Starting with the Am CAGED shape, here they are, ascending up the neck.

We began with the Am shape, so the CAGED order for these shapes is Am – G –Em – Dm – Cm.

Remember, the word CAGED starts over, so the Cm shape always follows the Dm shape, etc.

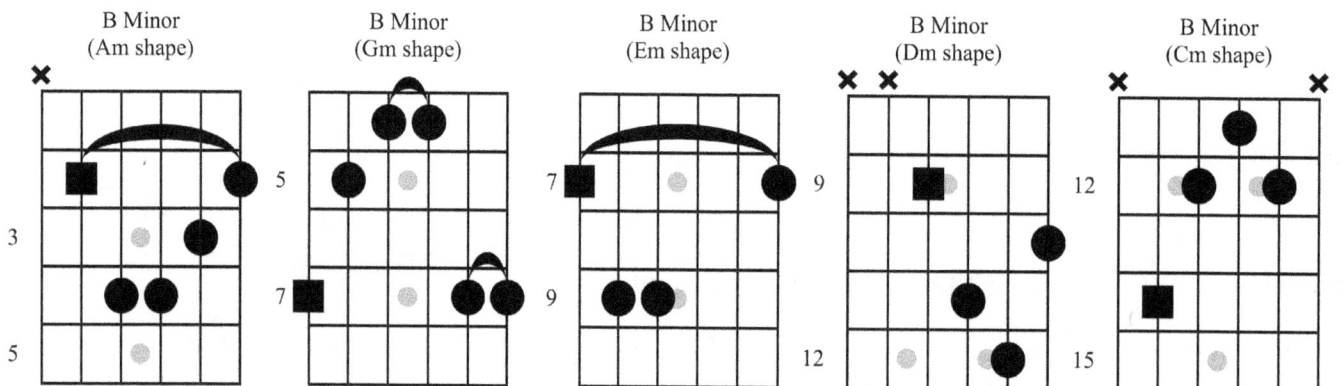

B Minor (Am shape) — B Minor (Gm shape) — B Minor (Em shape) — B Minor (Dm shape) — B Minor (Cm shape)

Example 6d:

Combining B minor CAGED shapes

Here is an example of playing a B minor chord which combines fragments of all five CAGED shapes and adds some embellishments. This idea would sit perfectly in a contemporary pop tune.

Example 6e:

Chapter Seven: Applying CAGED Minor Chords

Combining two minor chords

Now that you have an understanding of the minor CAGED chord forms and can see the smaller triads within the larger shapes, let's start making music with them by moving between Dm and Am chords in different places on the neck.

First, we'll identify some areas where we can play these chords, keeping them closely connected, then we'll explore adding embellishments and play a popular minor chord progression.

Dm to Am played on the first, second and third strings using CAGED Am and Em shapes

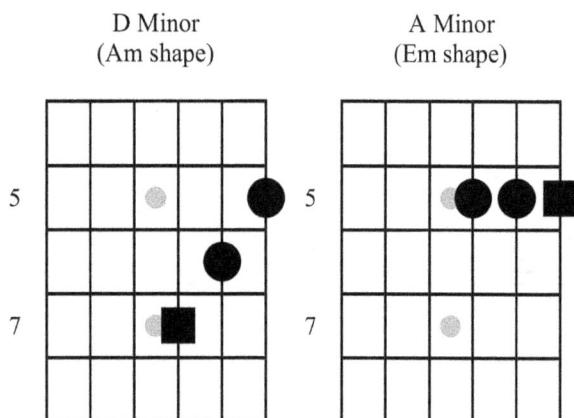

D Minor
(Am shape)

A Minor
(Em shape)

Here's a way to move from Dm to Am using chord voicings arranged on the top three strings. The A note on the first string is common to both voicings and helps them to sound connected.

Example 7a:

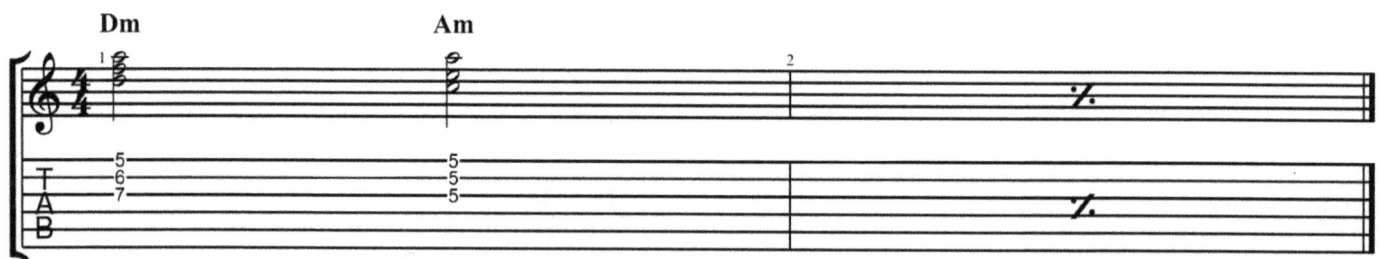

Dm to Am played on the fourth, fifth and sixth strings using CAGED Cm and Gm shapes

D Minor
(Cm shape)

A Minor
(Gm shape)

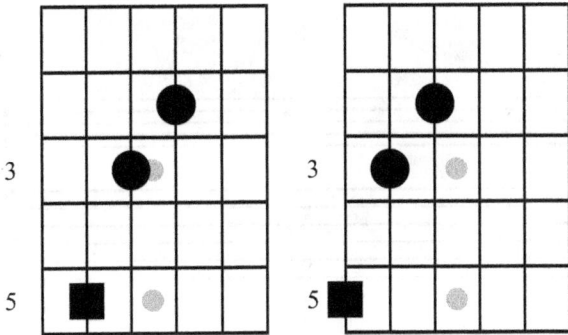

Using the Cm and Gm CAGED shapes, notice how the voicing is exactly the same for both chords, just played on a different string set.

Example 7b:

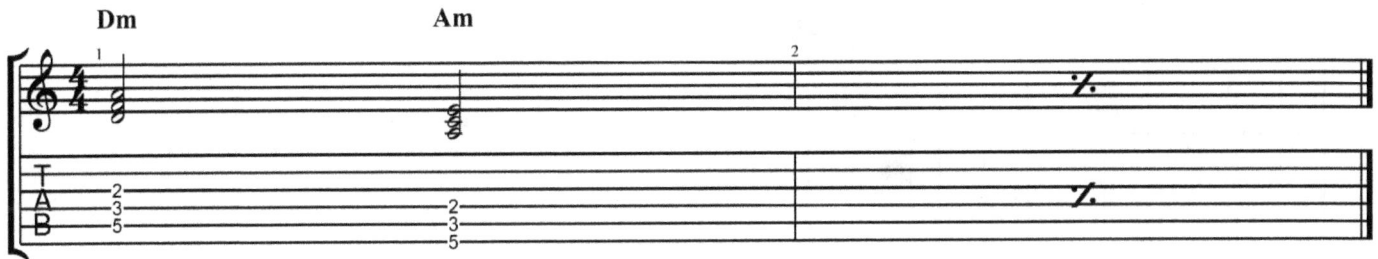

Dm to Am played on the second, third and fourth strings using CAGED Em and Cm shapes

D Minor
(Em shape)

A Minor
(Cm shape)

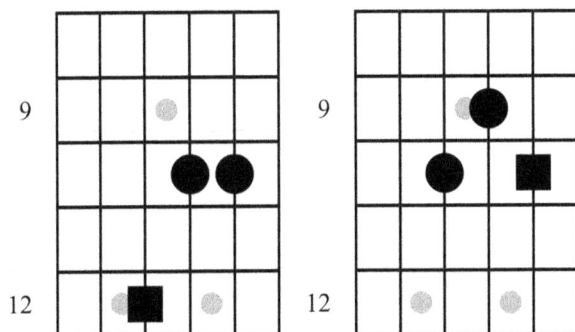

In this combination, notice how the notes descend on the third and fourth strings as we move from the Dm to Am chord, while the note on the second string remains constant. When used as part of a longer chord progression, this could be considered *voice leading* (where a melody line moves through the chords).

Example 7c:

Dm to Am played on the first, second and third strings using CAGED Dm and Am shapes

Voicings played on the top three strings, with no open strings or bass note, always work well for guitar parts. They cut through a band mix and don't conflict with the sonic range of the bass player.

Example 7d:

Make yourself a crib sheet of the CAGED shapes for both D minor and A minor chords then dedicate a practice session to switching between them in different zones of the neck. Come up with as many combinations as you can.

Chapter Eight: Adding Embellishments to CAGED Minor Chords

As we saw with major chords, one of the most useful elements of the CAGED system is the ability it gives us to play smaller fragments of chords that spell out the harmony while allowing embellishments to be added around them. We embellish these stripped-down voicings to suit a wide range of musical genres and create rhythm parts that can greatly enhance a song.

Let's examine some common embellishments to CAGED minor chords.

Adding extensions: the funky pinky

Take, for example, the way we played Dm and Am on the top three strings using CAGED Am and Em shapes. If we engage the funky pinky finger, we can create a hip line around both chords.

By playing the notes B and C on top of the Dm chord (with, you guessed it, the pinky) we are adding the 6th and b7th. Against the Am chord, we are adding the 9th.

However, you can just experiment with moving your pinky around, grabbing notes on the first string, to hear what you like the sound of. Try to continue a melodic idea from the Dm chord into the Am chord.

As well as adding extensions to the chords on the first string, varying where the chord is played against different beats (syncopation) helps to create a memorable guitar part. This is the kind of thing you might hear in a funky track by Prince.

D Minor   A Minor
(Am shape)   (Em shape)

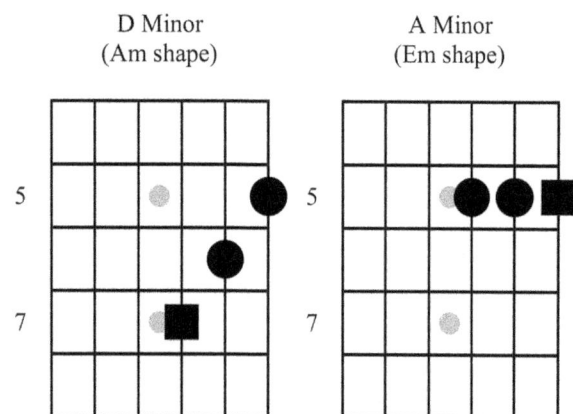

Example 8a:

3rd's as double-stops

If we revisit the Dm to Am movement played on the lower strings using CAGED Cm and Gm shapes, we can incorporate some 3rd's played as double-stops.

D Minor
(Cm shape)

A Minor
(Gm shape)

The double-stop notes come from the D Natural Minor scale (D E F G A Bb C). Play through them in this exercise below (there is no audio for this).

D Natural minor 3rd's as double-stops

3rds are incredibly helpful to create melodic parts that connect together chords. In Example 8b, the Am chord is played on beat 3& of bar one, then the Dm chord in bar two comes in on beat 1&. Adding syncopation like this can give a simple guitar part more impact. This idea has a Curtis Mayfield-style soulful vibe.

Example 8b:

Sliding 4th's

If we revisit Dm to Am played on the second, third and fourth strings using CAGED Em and Cm shapes, we can extract some 4th's, again played as double-stops. You can view these as being derived from the D Minor Pentatonic scale (D F G A C), based around the CAGED Em shape. The slides in and out of the 4th's add some fluidity to the sound.

Here's a reminder of the shapes and the D Minor Pentatonic shape used for embellishments.

D Minor Pentatonic Scale (CAGED Em Shape)

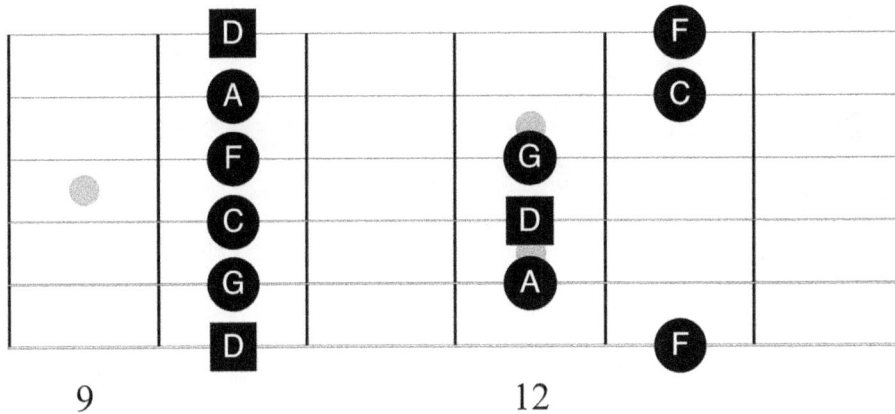

Here's an idea that could be adapted for use in a wide range of styles.

Example 8c:

Suspended chords

Look at the way we played the Dm to Am chord movement on the top three strings using the movable CAGED Dm and Am forms – the equivalents of their open chord voicings.

By moving the flattened third of the chords up to a fourth or down to a second, we can imply suspended chord sounds. These can be played as the chord rings out, or in single-note lines that connect the chords. Arpeggiating these ideas helps create a compelling rhythm guitar part that could be the main riff of a tune.

D Minor
(Dm shape)

A Minor
(Am shape)

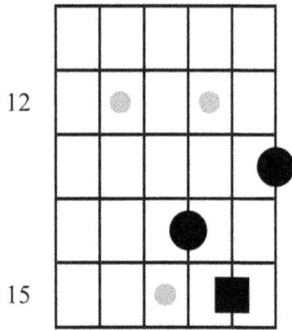

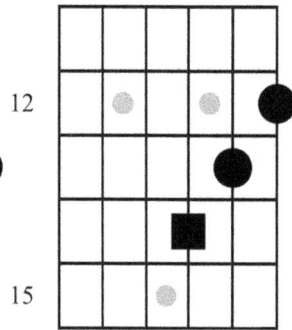

Example 8d:

Popular song form: the minor iv-v-i sequence

As we've been working on transitioning between Dm and Am chords, let's add a third minor chord (Gm) to create a popular chord progression – the minor iv-v-i.

Let's apply what we've learned so far, play the chords in several areas of the neck, and add some embellishments.

Here are the shapes, ranging from the 3rd to 8th fret.

G Minor
(Em shape)

A Minor
(Em shape)

D Minor
(Am shape)

G Minor
(Cm shape)

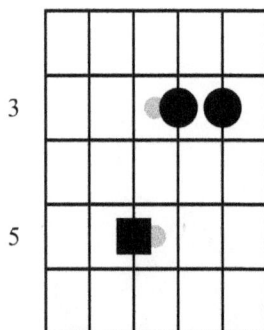

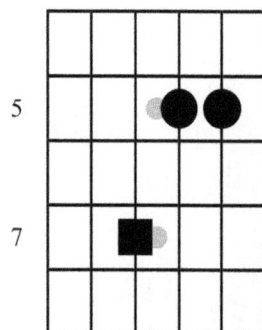

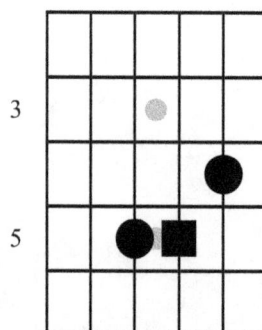

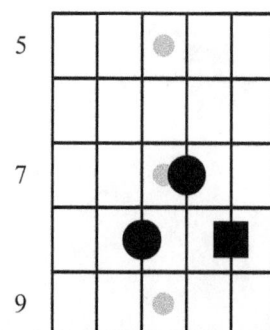

In Example 8e, notice how the first time through the chords the CAGED Em shape is used for both Gm and Am chords, then on the second time we switch to using the Cm shape for the Gm chord. Having these voicings under your fingers means you can vary your rhythm part in the moment, which is a very rewarding way to play guitar!

Example 8e:

Let's play the minor iv-v-i, this time in the 10th to 15th fret range.

Based around 10th position, this time you'll use the CAGED Am shape for Gm, the Cm shape for Am, and the Em shape for Dm. The embellishments were created using 3rds and 4ths, playing the fills mostly two notes at a time. Notice the Hendrix-style hammer-ons based around the CAGED Em shape for the Dm chord, extracted from the D Minor Pentatonic scale.

In this example, the iv (Gm) and v (Am) chords are played both in the same measure, with the i (Dm) in the second measure. Be sure to experiment like this, varying the duration of chords in your progressions, making some longer than others – it will inspire different rhythmic ideas.

Example 8f:

Chapter Nine: Combining CAGED Major & Minor Chords

As most songs combine major and minor chords, let's now apply our CAGED knowledge to several chord progressions that contain both chord types and play them in different areas of the neck.

Descending from A (second, third and fourth strings)

We'll use this common chord progression: A – E – Em – D – Bm – F#m – E

And we'll play it arranged on the second, third and fourth strings.

The diagrams show the full CAGED chords that we are deriving the the smaller voicings from.

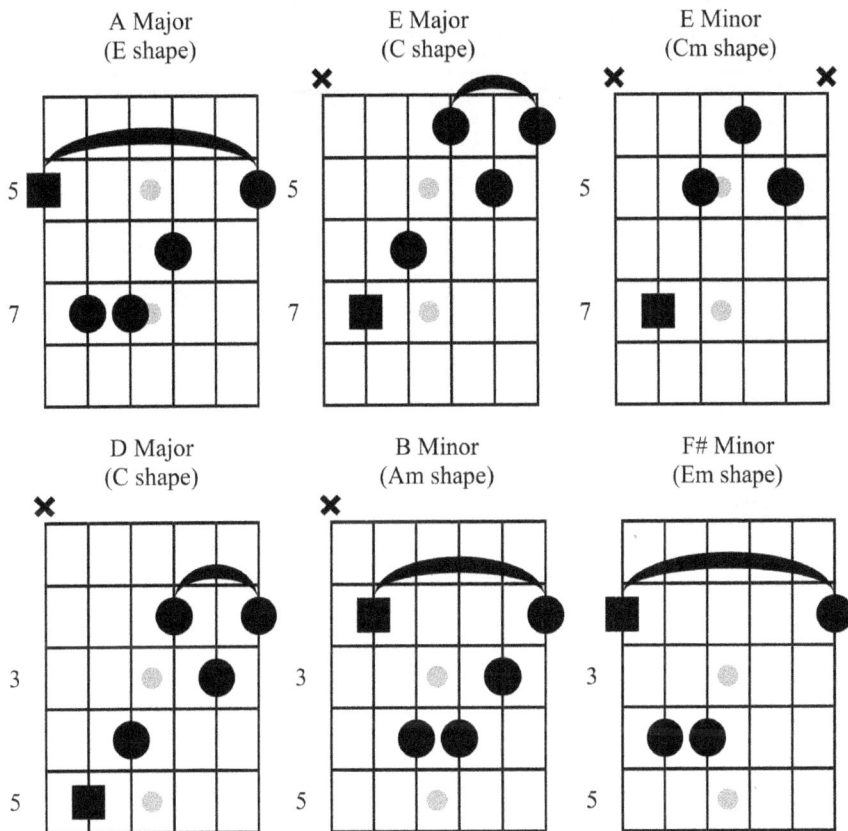

Notice the voice leading on the fourth string as the root note of the A chord descends through each chord, pulling the listener in. This type of voice leading is often heard in popular music, just listen to The Beatles!

Example 9a:

Descending from A (first, second and third strings)

Let's take the same chord progression but move it up the neck and play it now on the first, second and third strings.

The diagrams show the full CAGED chords that the smaller voicings come from.

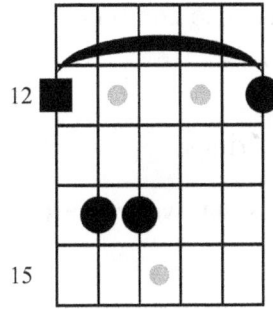

A Major (A Shape) · E Major (E Shape) · E Minor (Em Shape) · D Major (E Shape) · B Minor (Dm Shape) · F# Minor (Am Shape)

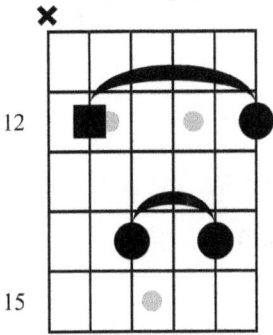

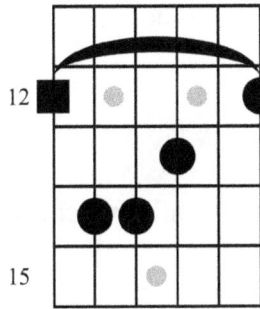

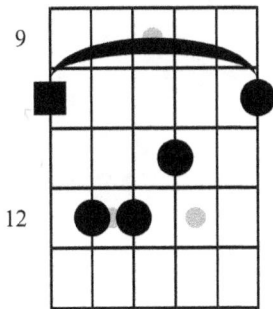

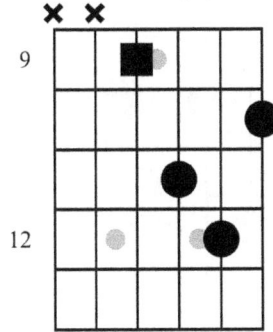

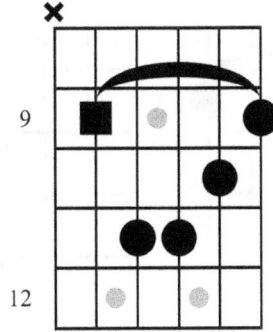

Notice that, this time, the voice leading occurs on the third string descending through the chords. The use of double-stops in the second half of the progression add some melodic movement to connect the chords.

Example 9b:

Ascending from B minor (first, second, third strings)

Let's take a different chord progression that also combines major and minor chords:

Bm – G – Em – A – F#m – F#

We'll play it on the first, second and third strings.

The diagrams show the full CAGED chords that we are deriving the smaller voicings from.

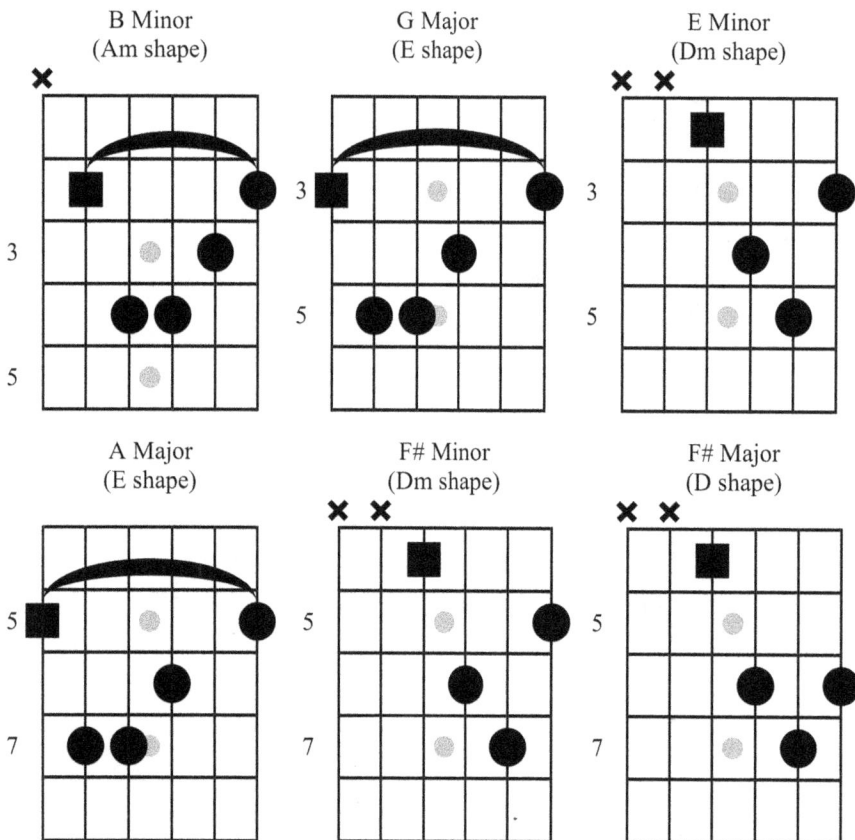

B Minor (Am shape) — G Major (E shape) — E Minor (Dm shape) — A Major (E shape) — F# Minor (Dm shape) — F# Major (D shape)

Notice that by splitting the chord and bass note we can simulate the sound of a piano. CAGED-based rhythm playing is often described as *pianistic*.

Example 9c:

Ascending from B minor (second, third and fourth strings)

Now, let's take the same chord progression and move it up the neck. This time we'll play it on the second third and fourth strings, adding embellishments. The diagrams show the full CAGED chord shapes.

B Minor
(Em shape)

G Major
(C shape)

E Minor
(Am shape)

A Major
(C shape)

F# Minor
(Cm shape)

F# Major
(C shape)

Notice how extensions are added to the chords Raising the root note by a whole step is an effective device to create movement around a chord. This is possible when using smaller voicings, as we are only playing three strings and we're not locked into a barre chord.

Example 9d:

Chapter Ten: Identifying CAGED Dominant 7th Chords

Now let's shift our attention to locating another popular chord type using the CAGED system: dominant 7th chords. These chords contain a major triad and a flattened 7th degree, which means we can build on our existing knowledge of CAGED major chord voicings.

Once again, each open chord shape (C7, A7, G7, E7, D7) represents a moveable chord form, so be sure to visualize these dominant 7th chords in the open position as we move them up the neck.

CAGED C7 shape

Let's look at how we can play a D7 chord using a CAGED C7 shape.

By relocating the note on the third string from the 2nd to the 5th fret, played with the fourth finger, we add the b7 note and turn a major chord into a dominant 7.

A quick way of locating the b7 is to remember that it is always a whole step below the root note of the chord. So, here the b7 is a C note, a whole step below the root note of D7.

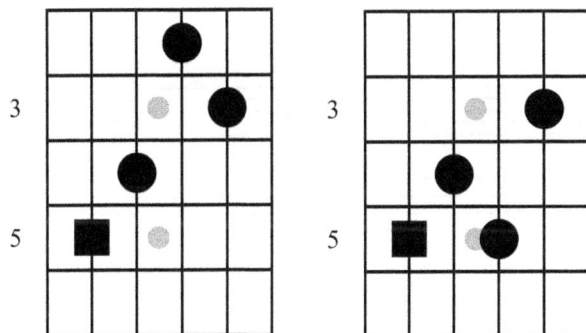

Example 10a:

CAGED A7 shape

When we play an open A7 shape the first, third and fifth strings are played open. Therefore, we need to use a barre as we move up the neck. To play D7, the first finger barres the 5th fret, beginning from the root note (D) on the fifth string. Notice that we include the b7 (C), located on the third string, as part of the barre.

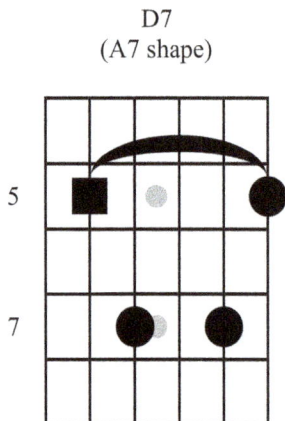

D7
(A7 shape)

Example 10b:

CAGED G7 Shape

When we play an open G7 shape, the second, third and fourth strings are played open, so we need to use a partial barre to make the shape moveable, as we did when playing the G major CAGED shape.

This time the second finger plays the b7 C note on the 8th fret, while the first finger barres the top four strings. Use your fourth finger to play the D root note on the sixth string, 10th fret, and your third finger for the F# note on the fifth string, 9th fret. If that feels too much like a finger gymnastics challenge, you can always omit the F# and mute the fifth string – the F# note also appears on the second string.

Don't worry about the stretches either, because in real world use, just the first four strings are often utilized for this voicing.

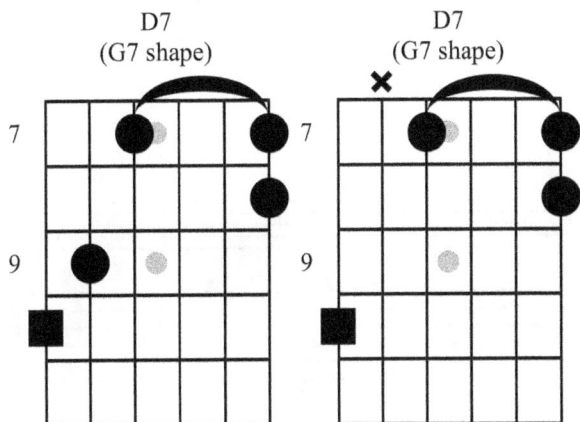

D7
(G7 shape)

D7
(G7 shape)

Example 10c:

CAGED E7 Shape

To make the E7 shape moveable, the first finger is used to barre the strings. The D root note is located at the 10th fret on the sixth string, and the ♭7 (C) is located on the fourth string as part of the barre. It can also be added on the second string, 13th fret.

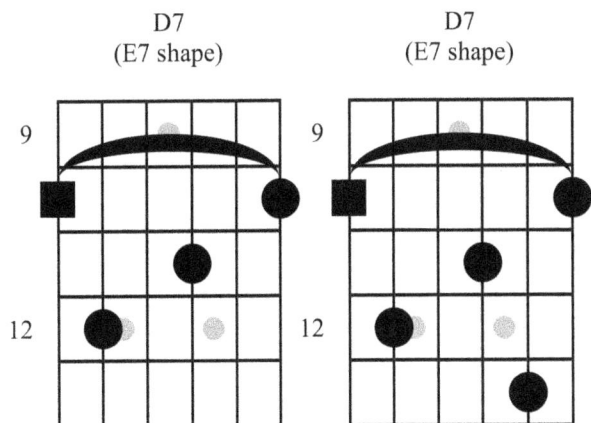

D7
(E7 shape)

D7
(E7 shape)

Example 10d:

CAGED D7 Shape

D7 played at the 12th fret shows the moveable version of the open D7 chord.

This one looks like a backward D triad, as we need to accommodate the b7 note (C on the second string, 13th fret). When we play an open D7 chord, the fourth string is played open, but in the moveable shape the first finger plays the D root note on the fourth string.

D7
(E7 shape)

Example 10e:

Finding inversions inside the shapes

Now we've played a D7 chord in five positions on the fretboard, let's investigate some of the musical possibilities that exist inside the shapes.

CAGED C7 shape: root triad and inversions

Let's return to the CAGED C7 shape for D7, but this time break it down into smaller shapes across groups of three strings. As before, these smaller shapes are all found inside the larger shape. D7 is constructed using the notes D, F#, A and C (respectively the root, 3rd, 5th and b7 intervals of the chord).

Starting from the fifth string root note, the first three-note shape forms a D7 triad with the notes D, F# and C, omitting the 5th. The 5th doesn't define the quality of the chord, so can be left out. As long as we have the 3rd and b7, the chord quality can be identified as a dominant 7.

If we move across a string and play the next three notes, beginning from the fourth string, we're playing a first inversion of D7. Here, the note order is F#, C, D (3rd, b7, 5th). This voicing is ideal for funk or blues, as it's a tight sounding chord that doesn't get in the way of the bass player.

If we move over a string to play the next group of three notes, we get a third inversion (a chord in which the b7 is the lowest note). Here, the note order is C, D, A. This voicing implies D7 but is less bluesy sounding, as the 3rd is omitted. This works well for more atmospheric situations. Think U2 or perhaps a prog-rock anthem!

Play through these shapes and fret/sound only the three notes in each chord, making sure to mute the other strings when picking or strumming. You'll need to use different fingers for these shapes, compared to the larger shape. The aim is to be able to switch between these smaller shapes while still visualizing the larger shape they came from.

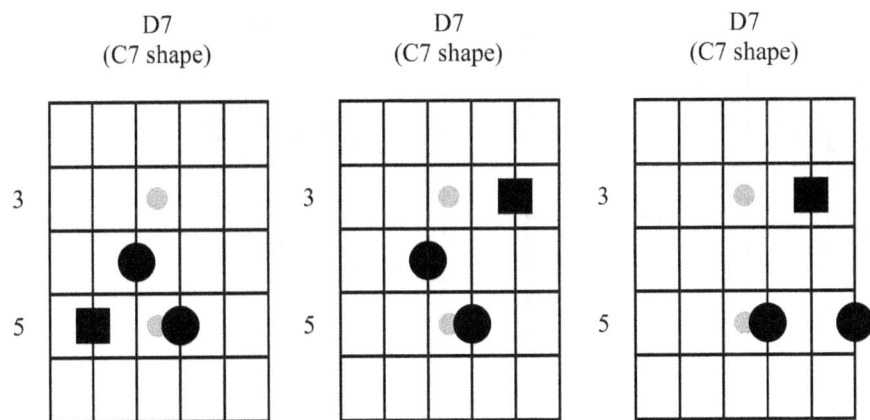

D7
(C7 shape)

D7
(C7 shape)

D7
(C7 shape)

Example 10f:

CAGED A7 shape: root triad and inversions

Let's apply the same idea to the CAGED A7 shape and play a D7 chord on groups of three strings.

If we begin by playing the chord from the root note on the fifth string, we get a D7 chord with no 3rd, which makes it less bluesy and more open sounding. This one shows up in Black Sabbath's *War Pigs*.

Playing the second, third and fourth strings yields a nice second inversion bluesy voicing.

The root triad begins on the third string and doesn't have the b7, although you could drop the root to the b7 as an alternative voicing.

Finally, this third inversion triad with the b7 (C) as its lowest note is a useful shape for intros or second guitar parts. Add some chorus or delay (or both) and experiment.

Example 10g:

Combining CAGED C7 and A7 shapes

Here are two examples of playing a D7 chord combining C7 and A7 shapes and adding some embellishments. Look at how the shapes are located next to each other on the fretboard. Get used to playing fragments of the chord shapes as you did with the major and minor CAGED shapes.

First, an ascending idea.

Example 10h:

Using voicings on the lower strings to begin with can help to create riff-like ideas.

Example 10i:

CAGED G7 shape: root triad and inversions

Now let's examine the CAGED G shape.

If we begin by playing a three-note chord from the D root on the sixth string we get a D triad, which forms the bottom part of the G shape. As an alternative, we can include the b7 on the fourth string, which creates a D7 triad, omitting the 5th (D, F#, C), as shown in the second grid in the diagram below.

If we play the chord from the fifth string, we get a first inversion with the 3rd (F#) in the bass.

The third inversion voicing, played on the second, third and fourth strings, is incredibly useful and may go down as the ultimate secret CAGED voicing! The b7 is played with the fourth finger on the fourth string, while the root and 3rd can be barred with the first finger across the second and third strings. This one is funky, bluesy, jazzy… what more can we ask from a three-string chord?! It fits perfectly around other instruments, so whether you play in a trio or a 10-piece band, keep this one in your chord arsenal.

Finally, the first, second and third strings yield a root–3rd–b7 voicing which can add a nice funky top end to your rhythm parts and shows up in a lot of blues tunes. This is because the 3rd and b7 are featured in the higher range, which is the foundation of the blues sound.

Example 10j:

D   D7   D7/F♯   D7/C   D7

CAGED E7 shape: root triad and inversions

For the E7 CAGED shape, if we begin by playing the D7 chord from its root note on the sixth string, we get a D7 triad with the 3rd (F#) omitted.

Playing from the fifth string yields a second inversion with the 5th (A) in the bass.

The third inversion voicing played on the second, third and fourth strings, with the b7 (C) in the bass, is a very useful voicing, especially when playing in jazz and blues contexts.

Finally, we have a first inversion with the 3rd (F#) as the lowest note, and by adding the b7 on the second string we have the vital ingredients of the dominant 7th chord. As a second guitar part, this voicing perfectly complements a dominant chord played in the lower register or in the open position.

D7 (E7 shape)   D7 (E7 shape)   D7 (E7 shape)   D7 (E7 shape)

Example 10k:

Combining CAGED G7 and E7 shapes

Now we'll play a D7 chord by combining CAGED G7 and E7 shapes and adding some embellishments. As with the G and E major CAGED shapes, notice how the G7 shape and E7 shape are located next to each other on the fretboard. Get used to playing fragments of these chord shapes.

Here's a swampy New Orleans blues-type lick using these shapes.

Example 10l:

And one more blues-infused idea.

Example 10m:

CAGED D7 shape: root triad and inversions

The lower register of the CAGED D shape isn't part of the open shape, but I'm adding it below as it's useful to help you visualize the full range of the D7 chord in a movable position.

Playing this three-note voicing from the sixth string gives us a first inversion with the 3rd (F#) in the bass.

Played from the fifth string, the shape yields a third inversion with the b7 (C) in the bass, omitting the 3rd. It's a subtle variation of the typical dominant 7th chord.

If we play a voicing from the fourth string we get another D7 chord without the 3rd, although this one implies the full chord as your ear tends to fill in the missing note. Fascinating!

Beginning a D7 voicing on the third string yields a popular blues triad form with the 5th (A) in the bass – a second inversion. This three-string voicing is easier to move up and down the neck, rather than playing the full CAGED D7 shape, which is why being able to quickly visualize these voicings is so important. This triad can be found everywhere. Think Delta blues tunes and Jimi Hendrix's *Red House*, as well as lots of funk and pop/rock songs.

Example 10n:

D7/F#   D7/C (no 3rd)   D7 (no 3rd)   D7/A

```
T|------------------------------------------------14----|
A|------------------13----------------13-----------13----|
B|------12----------14----------------14-----------14----|
 |------15----------12----------------12----------------|
 |------14----------15----------------------------------|
```

Combining CAGED dominant 7 shapes

Now we can begin to combine elements of all five CAGED shapes to play a D7 chord, adding some embellishments.

D7   D7   D7   D7   D7
(C7 shape) (A7 shape) (G7 shape) (E7 shape) (D7 shape)

This idea moves through different voicings of a D7 chord with arpeggiated inversions ascending up the neck, ending with a hammer-on to the major 3rd of the D7 chord (F#).

Example 10o:

D7

let ring - - - - - -| *let ring - - - - - - - -|*

```
T|--------3----3-------------7-----------7---------------13--12------10------|
A|------5----5------------5--------7--7--7---------14--12----10--11----------|
B|----0----4----4------7-------7--7--9--10-----12--12----10-----------------|
 |--3-------------------------9--------------------------------------------|
```

80

After sliding into the top three notes of the D7 shape, this line uses a phrase in 6ths in bar one to connect to the lower voicings.

Example 10p:

CAGED dominant 7th chords in another key

As with major and minor CAGED chords, you need to be able to transpose CAGED dominant 7th chords to different keys.

We've worked through this process twice already, so after learning the dominant 7 chord inversions and seeing the way they connect, you should be able to find the CAGED shapes and pick out the smaller voicings for a dominant 7 chord in another key.

Here are the large CAGED shapes for an A7 chord. Repeat the process we've used before to break apart the shapes and the three-note voicings contained in the larger form.

Example 10q:

Chapter Eleven: Applying CAGED Dominant 7th Chords

Combining two dominant 7 chords

Now that you have an understanding of the CAGED dominant 7 chord forms across the neck, it's time to work on combining them. You could use these voicings when playing blues changes, as the chords are generally all played as dominant 7s.

First, we'll identify some areas where we can play these chords keeping them closely connected, then we'll explore adding embellishments, as we did with major and minor CAGED shapes.

C7 to F7 played on the first, second and third strings using CAGED A7 and D7 shapes

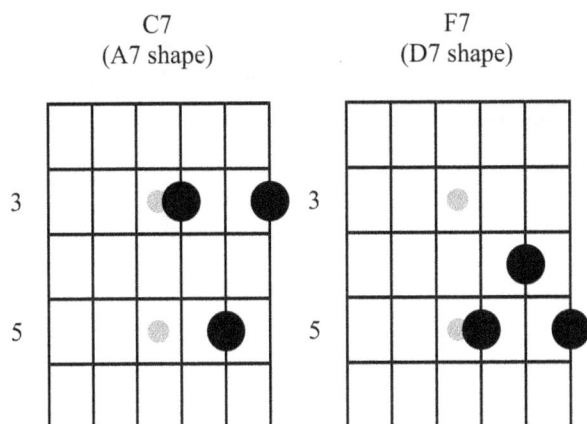

C7
(A7 shape)

F7
(D7 shape)

When playing the C7 to F7 progression using A7 and D7 CAGED shapes on the top three string, notice the movement of the note E to Eb on the second string. This is the 3rd of C7 moving to the b7 of the F7. This resolution is a common movement found throughout blues changes.

Example 11a:

C7 to F7 played on the second, third and fourth strings using CAGED G7 and C7 shapes

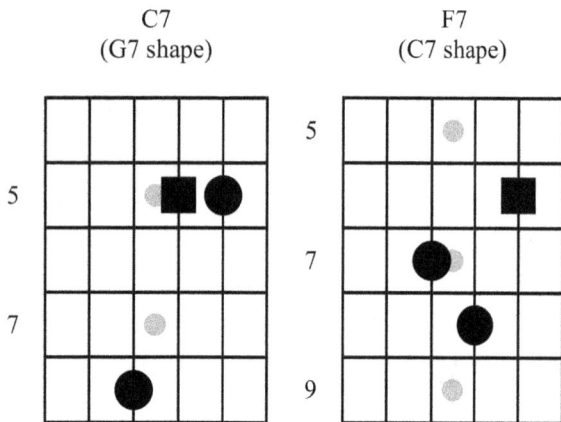

C7
(G7 shape)

F7
(C7 shape)

Next, using these shapes, notice that the b7 of the C7 chord (Bb) on the fourth string, moves down a half-step to the 3rd of the F7 chord (A). Again, this is fundamental movement in the blues and when voiced like this, it ensures that the chords sound connected.

Example 11b:

C7 to F7 played on the first, second and third strings using CAGED E7 and A7 shapes

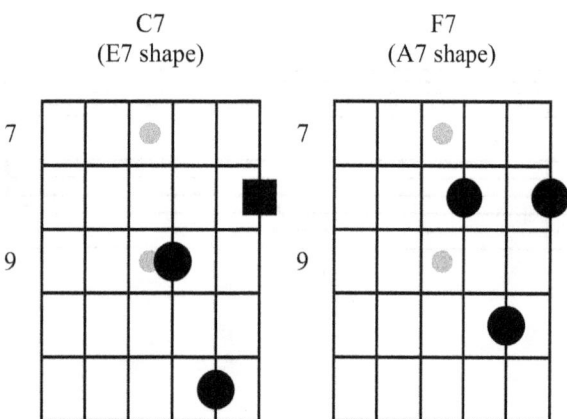

C7
(E7 shape)

F7
(A7 shape)

For this C7 chord we are utilizing the E7 CAGED voicing where the b7 (Bb) is played on the second string.

Playing these chords on the top three strings gives them a chiming, ringing quality, and is ideal for intros and second guitar parts, especially if you experiment with rhythm or add some effects.

Example 11c

C7 to F7 played on the fourth, fifth and sixth strings using CAGED D7 and G7 shapes

As you've probably noticed, I tend to think that the middle and top three strings are the most useful for CAGED voicings. However, just to show you that another string set can be utilized, here I'm using the three lowest strings to move between C7 and F7. Synth-based electronic bands often use this register of the guitar, so be sure to experiment on all string sets.

Example 11d:

C7 to F7 played on the second, third and fourth strings using CAGED D7 and G7 shapes

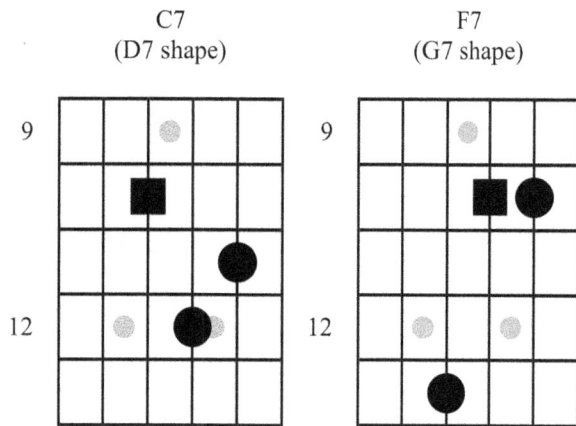

C7
(D7 shape)

F7
(G7 shape)

Here is C7 to F7 based on the same CAGED shapes as the previous example, but this time played on the second, third and fourth strings.

Example 11e:

Now you've learned some useful voicings to transition between C7 and F7, go back and experiment with the shapes and see what other ways you can find.

Chapter Twelve: Adding Embellishments to CAGED Dominant 7th Chords

We know that adding tasteful embellishments is the way to bring our rhythm guitar playing to life, so let's examine how we can embellish CAGED dominant 7th chords.

Chordal lines

Let's revisit the way we played C7 to F7 on the top three strings using CAGED A7 and D7 shapes. By arpeggiating the chords and adding a 6th to each shape (C and D respectively) we can create a musical line that connects the chords and forms a melodic part, rather than just strumming away.

Hold down the chord shapes and allow the notes to ring into each other as you pick them out, as this provides a full sound. Notice that we begin by playing 1/8th notes, then switch to 1/16th notes at the end of the second measure. Adding some rhythmic variation to your guitar parts is a tried and tested way to keep them interesting.

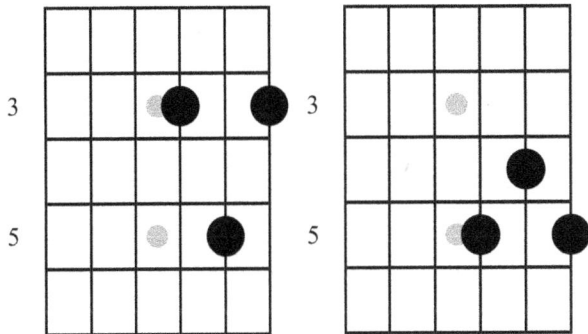

C7
(A7 shape)

F7
(D7 shape)

Example 12a

Mixolydian licks

If we revisit C7 to G7 played on the second, third and fourth strings using CAGED G7 and C7 shapes, we can add some single-note ideas based on the C Mixolydian scale (C D E F G A Bb).

C Mixolydian is the fifth mode of the harmonized F Major scale and perfectly fits over a C7 chord, containing the root, 3rd, 5th and b7. See the scale diagram below.

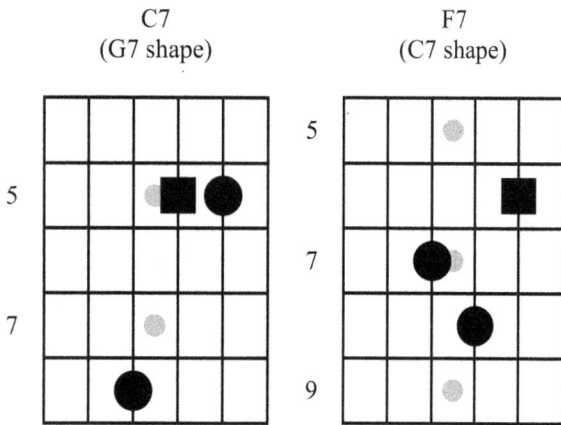

C Mixolydian (CAGED G7 Shape)

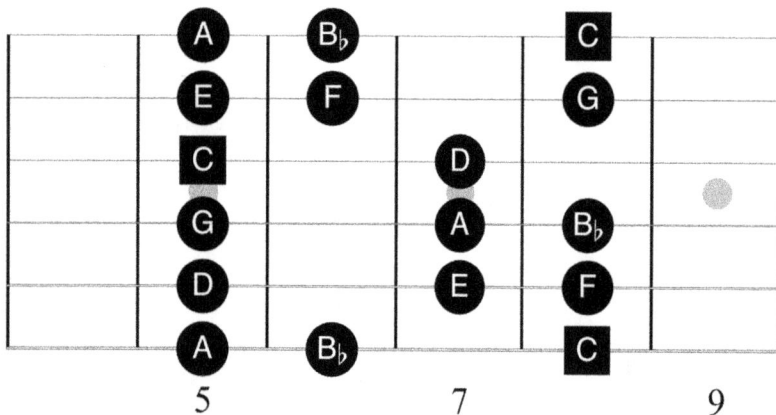

The Mixolydian is ideal for conjuring up bluesy lines, as in Example 12b.

Example 12b:

Getting funky!

C7
(E7 shape)

F7
(A7 shape)

Let's revisit the C7 to F7 change using E7 and A7 CAGED shapes arranged on the top three strings. These voicings are ideal for some funky rhythm playing.

We can create a little movement by adding a 9th (D) to the C7 chord, and by raising the 3rd of the F7 chord to a 4th (A to Bb).

By adding syncopation in the picking hand to accent chords on different beats, we can create some memorable funky motifs. Once you have this down you just need to find a good hat and some bell bottoms!

Example 12c

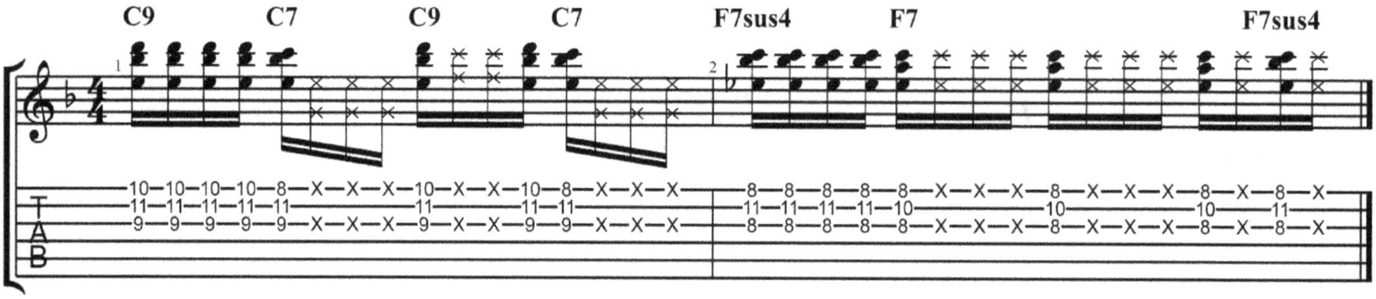

Combining 3rds and 4ths as double-stops

Let's play C7 with the CAGED D7 shape, and F7 voiced using the CAGED G7 shape, both arranged on the second, third and fourth strings.

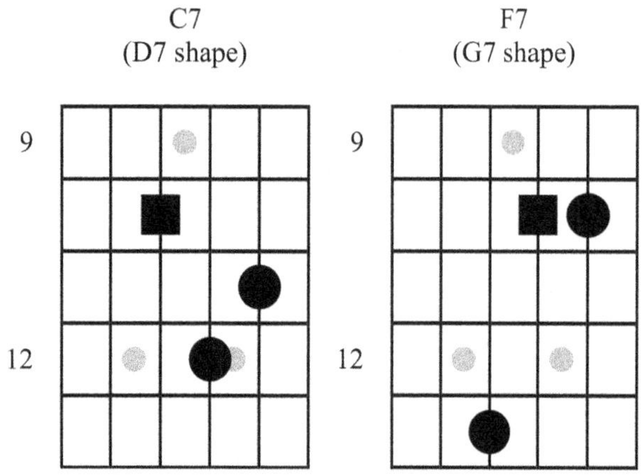

C7
(D7 shape)

F7
(G7 shape)

Here we'll combine 3rds and 4ths played as double-stops to create a melodic part. The double-stops are taken from the C Mixolydian scale and based around the CAGED D7 and C7 shapes.

First play the following two exercises (there is no audio for these).

C Mixolydian in 3rds as double-stops

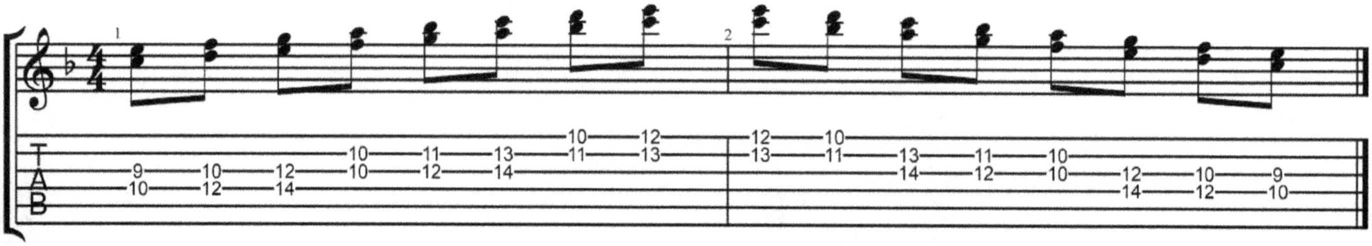

C Mixolydian in 4th's as double-stops

Now play the following idea connecting the two chords.

Example 12d:

Popular song form: the I-IV-V blues

A 12-bar blues in the key of C contains the chords C7, F7 and G7.

You should now be able to find a G7 chord in the same area of the neck as a C7 and an F7.

Here's a longer example of a 12-bar blues in C, using CAGED E7, A7 and C7 shapes.

In the 12th measure (the turnaround), I add a #9 and b9 to the G7 chord, which creates a tension that is resolved as the C7 chord comes around again at the start of the 12-bar form.

C7
(E7 shape)

F7
(A7 shape)

G7
(C7 shape)

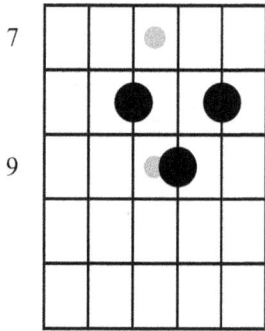 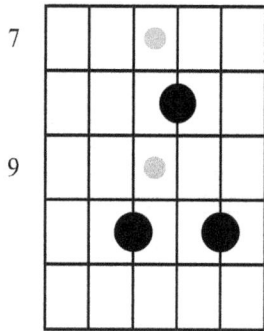 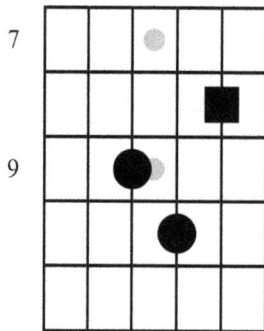

Example 12e:

Chapter Thirteen: Putting it All Together (I-vi-ii-V7)

The best way to practice CAGED rhythm playing is to apply what you're learned to songs/chord progressions. By working through the process of identifying the CAGED shapes, extracting smaller voicings and adding embellishments that fit the music, you'll become a more versatile and sophisticated rhythm player.

This should be your process:

1. Choose a key and a chord progression

Let's take a progression in the key of E Major as our example. We'll use the common sequence of I-vi-ii-V7. In the key of E Major, the chords will be:

E – C#m – F#m – B7

(To create your own progressions, a good place to start is by looking up the chords that belong to a major or minor key and selecting combinations of chords you like the sound of).

2. Choose an area of the neck and a string set

Let's head for the middle of the neck and see how this chord progression sounds voiced around the 4th to 7th fret. Our aim is to arrange the chord voicings on the top three strings.

The first thing we need to do is to locate the root note of each chord in that zone of the fretboard. With this information, we can begin to find the larger CAGED shapes that fit in that area of the neck.

As you become more familiar with seeing chord voicings on smaller string sets, you'll be able to skip this step and go straight to the voicing you want.

3. Play the shapes on a smaller string set

While visualizing the larger shapes, we want to work with the smaller shapes that exist within them. You can choose any string set for your explorations, but the most common are the top three strings or the second, third and fourth strings. You can also mix and match them and use the lower strings too. Here, we are aiming for an arrangement on the top three strings.

4. Add rhythm/embellishments

Once you have worked out the voicings on a smaller string set and can play them, it's time to experiment with *rhythm*. First, think about the way you are playing the chords. Varying the rhythmic feel can go a long way to creating an interesting part.

Next, you can add some embellishments. Let the music tell you what type of fills to add. It could be single-note lines, double-stops, slides, adding chord extensions… Think about the genre of music you are playing and be guided by what sounds good to you!

Be sure to experiment though. Sometimes these ideas come quickly and at other times they can take a while to reveal themselves. You'll know when you have a good part for the song.

It can be fun to come up with a few different genre variations of the same chord progression, so try that too!

5. Repeat the process in another area of the neck

Now choose another area of the neck, identify the larger CAGED shapes, find the smaller voicings within them on a different string set to before, and embellishments to them.

Be sure to repeat this exercise in different keys and with different chord progressions.

* * *

Now let's look at the solution to the example I proposed earlier: the I-vi-ii-V7 chord progression in the key of E Major, with the chords E – C#m – F#m – B7.

We need major, minor and dominant CAGED shapes in the middle zone of the neck. Here are the shapes:

CAGED shapes: E – C#m – F#m – B7 (4th-7th fret)

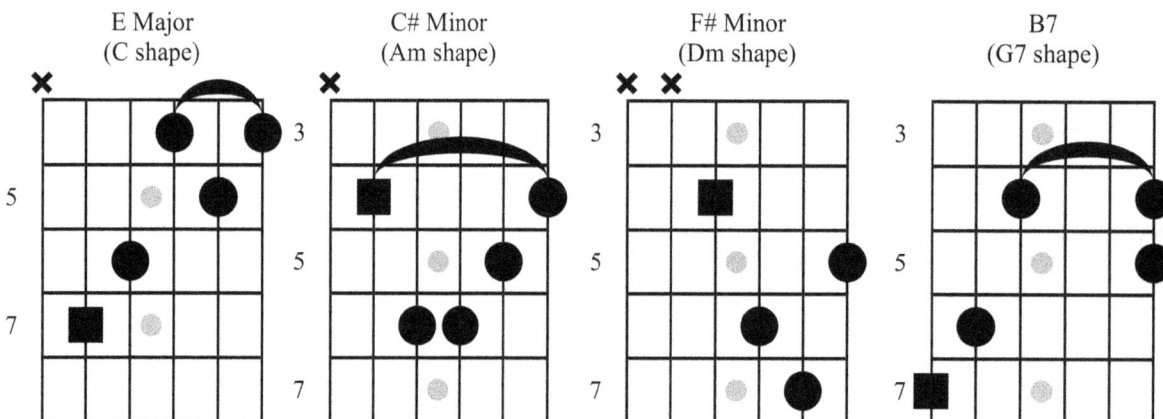

Take a moment to identify where the root notes of the chords sit and visualize each large CAGED shape that stems from it. In this zone of the neck, there is an E root note on the fifth string, 7th fret for the E major, chord, and a C# root note at the 4th from for the C# minor chord, etc.

Example 13a:

(Musical notation: chords E, C#m, F#m, B7 in standard notation and tablature)

Let's extract the top part of each large CAGED shape, so that we are playing voicings arranged on just the top three strings.

Example 13b:

(Musical notation: chords E, C#m, F#m, B7 in standard notation and tablature)

Now, we can begin to take creative decisions about *how* we want to play these voicings. In Example 13c I arpeggiated the melody and added some common tones and extensions. I wasn't really thinking about what notes to add, I just experimented and reached for what sounded good located next to the chord voicings until I came up with what sounded like a cohesive idea.

With these embellishments the chords ended up sounding a bit folky, or perhaps like the keyboard line from a progressive rock song.

Example 13c:

(Musical notation: arpeggiated passage over chords E, C#m, F#m, B7 with "let ring" indication, in standard notation and tablature)

Working in the same zone of the neck, we can now try a different approach by playing the voicings on the next string set (second, third and fourth strings).

Remember, we're using the same large CAGED shapes and position on the neck – we're just pulling out different small voicings.

Hammering onto the E chord from the 4th fret gives the opening a Rolling Stones vibe, and by playing the F#m chord on the second, third and fourth strings only, we end up with a power chord (F#5) as there is no 3rd, which adds to the rock!

For embellishment, I lowered and raised the 5th to create some movement within the chord. You might ask why I'm not playing F#m here? I played the F# chord as F#5 and liked it, so I kept it.

There really are no rules other than what you play should sound good to you, so go for it!

Example 13d:

Now, following our process, let's start over and move to a different location on the neck. Let's go higher and see what we can find in the fret 9-12 zone of the neck.

First look for the root notes of the chords. For the E major chord, it's got to be the sixth string root at the 12th fret, but for the other three chords, root notes can be found on the bottom three strings, all at the 9th fret.

From these root notes, build the appropriate large CAGED shapes.

Here are the big shapes I'm extracting the voicings from:

Here's a final embellishment example that sticks closely to these shapes, with the addition of some melodic 3rds in the second measure.

Example 13e:

More chord progressions

Be sure to experiment with other chord progressions and play in different keys to build your skills and chord visualization abilities.

Here are some popular chord progressions you can experiment with, written below in the key of E Major. (Remember our discussion about harmonizing scales into chords in Chapter Four?)

F#m – B7 – E (ii – V – I)

E – G#m – A – B7 (I – iii – IV – V7)

E – B7 – C#m – A (I – V7 – vi – IV)

E – C#m – A – B (I – vi – IV – V)

E – B – C#m – G#m – A – E – B7 (I – V7 – vi – iii – IV – I – V7)

Conclusion

Thanks for reading this book. I hope you feel as though we've unlocked the CAGED system together.

I hope you've enjoyed our journey and feel as though you have a better understanding of the fretboard, the notes on the neck, CAGED chords, and how to expand your rhythm playing.

The best way to practice this method is simply to apply it. Take a song you know the chords to and "CAGE" it!

Choose an area of the neck, find the CAGED chords, then experiment playing on smaller string sets, adding embellishments and don't forget to vary your rhythm.

Do this in different areas of the neck and you'll soon feel confident enough to perform that song on the fly, creating a rhythm part in real time.

Knowing CAGED voicings all over the neck and being able to see lines move through chord progressions is a big part of improvising through chord changes.

When you learn a new song or chord progression, put in the time it takes to get the chords under your fingers in different areas across the fretboard. Know the notes and see the inversions. You'll find your confidence as a player grows at a rapid rate by doing this.

Have fun, be musical and, most important of all, enjoy the journey!

Rob